MW00668466

IRONDALE CAFE · ORIGINAL
WHISTLE-STOP
TM
CAFE
COOKBOOK

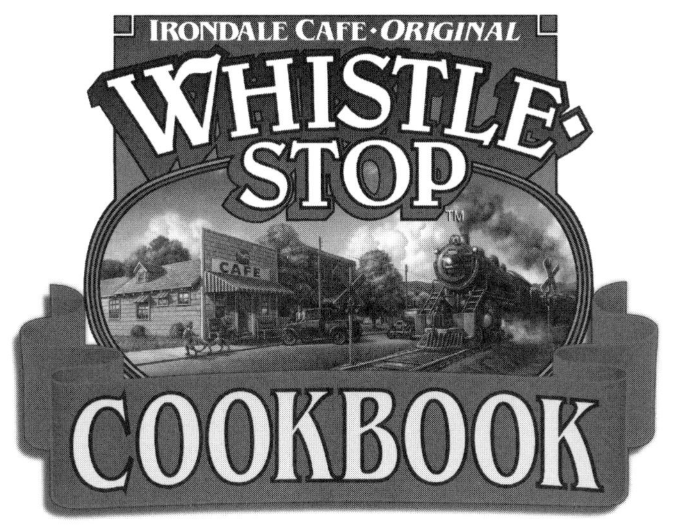

A Culmination of the History, Favorite Recipes, and Preparation Tips from the Irondale Cafe

by

Mary Jo Smith McMichael

with

Tips for Healthier Eating

by

Connie F. McMichael, MS, RD

Published by

CRANE HILL
PUBLISHERS
2923 Crescent Avenue • Birmingham, Alabama 35209

Printed in the United States of America
Published by Crane Hill Publishers

McMichael, Mary Jo, 1932 -
Irondale Cafe original whistle stop cookbook / Mary Jo Smith McMichael. — 1st ed.
p. cm.
ISBN 1-881548-66-X
1. Cookery. 2. Irondale Cafe. I. Title.
TX714.M387 1995
641.5—dc20 95-34649
CIP

Front cover photo: Sophia Marlowe
Book design by Bob Weathers and Scott Fuller

Crane Hill Publishers
www.cranehill.com

Table of Contents

Acknowledgements

I would like to acknowledge my immediate family: my husband, Billy, who has helped me a great deal before and since his retirement from the railroad; my son Bill, Jr., who has stood by me with encouragement and concern through the hard years and has helped tremendously in the production and release of this cookbook; my daughter Beth Nail, who as a teenager gave up so many Saturdays in order to help at the cafe and who has always been there for me; Beth's husband, Dwayne, who has assumed much of the workload and added so much humor to the everyday atrocities of work; my granddaughter, Brooke, who is such a delight to us, we love her so much; and my daughter Connie, who spent so much time alone during her childhood, but has grown up to be very close to us and who has proven herself with the success of her education. To my sisters, nieces, nephews, and extended family. You are all so special to me!

A Tribute to Fannie Flagg

In the mid-sixties, a young woman named Fannie Flagg became co-anchor of the morning show with Tom York. I would take my children to school and rush home to see her segment of the show. I thought she was so pretty and clever and I loved watching her. Of course, I had no idea how successful she would become.

In the early '80s, Fannie walked into my office and introduced herself. I was so excited! We chatted for quite a while and I felt as if I had known her forever.

A special acknowledgement to Fannie Flagg,
who has not only been a great inspiration,
but has brightened many days
with a phone call or a special note.

Dedication

This book is dedicated to the memory of my loved ones:

Mom, Mary Frances Alma Baker Smith; Dad, John William Smith, Sr.; Brother, J. W. Smith, Jr.; Sister, Ruth Evelyn Brown; my dear niece, Ann Brown Thomas; and my beloved niece and friend, Carol Donehoo Sanders.

Also to the memory of my husband's parents, Ina Belle Moore McMichael and Walstein Hilman McMichael, and his sister and brother-in-law, Elizabeth McMichael Taylor and Harry C. Taylor.

The love given to me by my loved ones has made me who I am today. They taught me many things and their actions gave me a direction to base my life; simply stated in the Bible verse Galatians 5:22,23:

"And the fruit of the spirit is love, joy,
peace, patience, kindness, goodness, faithfulness,
gentleness, and self-control."

Preface

In the fall of 1972, the unexpected happened. Never in my wildest dreams had I ever imagined running a restaurant. Of course, owning the Irondale Cafe wasn't my idea!

We baked a cake, and some folks in Juliette, Georgia, got the icing.

The author, Mary Jo McMichael, in front of the original Irondale Cafe building the day before it was torn down.

Mary Jo McMichael in front of the Irondale Cafe as it appears today.

Foreword

As you get close to the little town of Irondale, you begin to think back in time to the little community where most of us grew up. There are frame houses with an occasional brick house, children playing in well-groomed yards, and sidewalks with folks out for a stroll. There are well-landscaped knolls with trees, grass, and picket fences. As you near the old Main Street, there is evidence of old and new. As you approach the Original Whistle Stop Cafe, there is an air of yesteryear with shade trees close by and well-lit walkways leading to the cafe. Giant freight trains are often on the tracks not more than 60 feet away. When you walk into the front door there are people from all walks of life eating meals prepared with tender loving care. Most of them know the owners and refer to them as Mr. and Mrs. Mc. There are pictures of old Irondale and some of its famous people as well as paparazzi from the novel *Fried Green Tomatoes at the Whistle Stop Cafe*.

Also in view is a poster from the movie *Fried Green Tomatoes* that the owner of the cafe and most town folks are proud to be connected to, even in a small way. Customers enjoy this friendly down home atmosphere and good home cooking. As patrons enjoy their meal, there is always the nearby rumbling of a freight train. Customers young and old scramble to get seats near the windows to watch the trains. Afterward, folks gather around the little gift shop where various cafe delights, colorful gifts, and memorabilia can be bought. Many visit local shops while others sit on park benches and watch the trains, discuss the weather, politics, or even the recent additions to their families.

All in all, there is a down home and delicious combination of close families, good friends, and good food in a pleasant atmosphere of good times and special fellowship. I hope this book conveys the same warm atmosphere and provides you with some of our down home and delicious cuisine to share with your family and friends.

Mary Jo McMichael and husband Bill at the Irondale Cafe enjoying a home-cooked Whistle Stop meal.

CHAPTER 1

The Irondale Cafe

---

by

Mary Jo Smith McMichael

Maggie Prentice, one of the cafe's original owners, in 1932. Photo courtesy of Erma Knief.

From Hot Dogs to Full-Course Meals

The Irondale Cafe began in 1928 as a hot dog stand owned by Emmett Montgomery. Miss Bess Fortenberry purchased the business about 1932 from a woman named Maggie Prentice, who had added hamburgers, barbecue, and a variety of sandwiches to the menu. I'm not sure exactly when the "stand" was renamed the Irondale Cafe, but I think it was shortly after Bess took over.

Bess, who came from a prominent Irondale family, was single and had a great enthusiasm for life. She was free-hearted, loved practical jokes, and built a successful business.

In the early forties, Bess leased the Irondale Cafe and went to Florida to work for the war effort. While in Florida, she ran into an old acquaintance, Sue Lovelace. After the war, Bess convinced Sue and a wonderful cook, a black lady named Lizzie Cunningham, to come back to Irondale with her and help in the cafe.

The trio made the Irondale Cafe one of the most popular places around town to dine. They cooked such good vegetables and meats, and they had a thriving sandwich business. What made the sandwiches especially desirable was that they were made "to go"—primarily because there wasn't much room in the cafe for sit-down eating at that time.

In 1972, Bess suffered a light stroke and decided to sell the cafe and retire. About that time, Sue developed a severe case of shingles and was unable to continue working. Lizzie had diabetes and high blood pressure, and her doctor had told her to retire two or three years earlier.

Someone Else's Idea Becomes My Reality

I was unaware that my husband, Billy, had any interest in the Irondale Cafe until he started talking about buying it from Miss Bess Fortenberry in late November 1972. Billy had eaten lunch at the cafe on numerous occasions, but I had never been there and really didn't know much about Irondale. We had moved to the Roebuck-Huffman area of Birmingham from Atlanta in August 1963. Our children (Bill, Jr., Beth, and Connie) went to school near our house, and I did most of my shopping in nearby stores. All I really knew was that Southern Railway, the railroad company where Billy worked, was in Irondale.

When Billy talked to Bess about buying the cafe, she told him to have me come talk to her. I went to the cafe after lunch one day to talk with Bess and see the restaurant. I remember that when I walked in the front door, it was so dim inside that I could hardly see. A lady met me and took me back to the kitchen, where Bess was sitting on a stool drinking a cup of coffee. She introduced me to the workers who were standing nearby, and then she turned to me and said, "What in the world do you want to buy this cafe for?" I told her that it was my husband who wanted to buy it, but that I was willing to work with him. A lady who was working at the cafe had told Billy she would continue to work for us and she would just need me during lunch hour. I was really apprehensive about buying the cafe, but Billy was insistent.

Bess told me that another couple was anxious to buy the cafe, and she was going to decide who to sell it to after she talked to me. I went home that night and *prayed* that she would decide to sell it to the other couple because I surely didn't know anything about running a business. A few days later Billy came in from work and told me that Bess had decided to sell it to us. I was overwhelmed.

It was mid-December when we bought the Irondale Cafe. We spent all New Year's Day at the restaurant inventorying the stock, and at 5:30 a.m. January 2, 1973, we opened for business. I came in at 11 a.m. and worked through lunch. We had decided to open the cafe on Saturday, so both Billy and I came in at 5:30 the first Saturday morning. We had a smaller crew on Saturdays, and the two of us worked all day.

That Sunday night, our manager called to tell us she had the flu. She was so sick that she stayed home for three weeks. Thankfully, Bess stood by and helped me get through those weeks. When our manager did come back to work, she told me I would have to close in the afternoons because she just couldn't hold up to the long hours any longer—and she couldn't work on Saturdays. So I started working more hours.

We served a full breakfast six mornings a week, and a lunch menu six days a week, as well as sandwiches in the afternoons. We sold beer at the time and had a pretty lively late-afternoon business. We closed at 5 p.m., and two or three of us would do the prep work for the next day, finishing about 6:30.

Bursting at the Seams

When my husband and I bought the Irondale Cafe, it was housed in a small frame building with light-green siding trimmed in white. There was one step up to the entrance, which was in the middle of the front, with a single window on each side. The awning over the front had a big red Coca-Cola sign hanging above it.

Inside, the floors sprang with you when you walked. The front room had four booths lining the outer wall, small tables in the center of the room, and a long counter, with eight wooden and metal Coca-Cola stools, running from one front window back to the register. The back room had three booths and an old Rockola. The kitchen separated the two "dining" rooms.

The seating capacity for the front room was 31, and that was, as the old saying goes, "packed like sardines." One of the first things we did was take out the counter and put in more tables so we could comfortably seat more people.

Expanding the Menu

When we took over from Bess, the weekly menu was:

Monday: Meat loaf, turnip greens, large butter beans (dried), stewed potatoes, coleslaw, and cornbread

Tuesday: Roast beef, mashed potatoes, green beans, black-eyed peas, coleslaw, and cornbread

Wednesday: Turkey and dressing with giblet gravy and cranberry sauce, macaroni and cheese, Fordhook limas, coleslaw, and rolls (Bess said Wednesday's cornbread was in the dressing.)

Thursday: Fried pork chops, mashed potatoes and gravy, turnip greens, Great Northern beans, coleslaw, and cornbread

Friday: Beef stew, green beans, black-eyed peas, coleslaw, candied yams, and cornbread

There were no regular desserts, although occasionally Sue would make a few pies. The beverages were always tea, coffee, soft drinks, and beer. When you came in and sat down, you ordered either a regular lunch or a small lunch, the only difference being the size of the servings and about twenty-five cents in price.

If you didn't like the meat of the day, there was always baked ham or barbecue in the cooler. Barbecue was the favorite, followed by our regular hamburger, deluxe hamburger, hot dog, ham, BLT, and grilled cheese. (Our regular hamburger, which came with mustard, onions, and hot sauce, was the best hamburger I had ever eaten.)

We started serving at 11 a.m., and we would usually run out of food by 12:30, so we started cooking more of everything. When we closed for vacation the first week of July that first year, Billy and some friends installed a steam table so we could add more variety to the daily menu.

On Saturdays, we fried chicken, made hamburger steaks, fried okra, cabbage, French fries, tossed salad, and several vegetables. We started serving two or three meats daily, including the "meat of the day" from Bess' menu. Then we added several more vegetables, along with tossed salad, in addition to Bess' regular vegetables. We put in a "top of the line" packaged pie and started baking rolls every day in addition to cornbread. Eventually we added homemade desserts to the cobbler and ready-made ones.

Expanding the Building

We continued to operate in the little frame building until the end of 1979. During the summer of 1979, the Jefferson County Health Department started "getting in behind" all of the old, out-of-date buildings that housed restaurants. Our little building had been built in the late 1920s, and we really were out of date. When we had purchased the restaurant from Bess, however, we were told that all we had to do to meet the codes was to add a hand-washing sink in the kitchen.

We looked around and even talked with a man who had a beautiful lot for a restaurant, but there was a sewer moratorium at the time and we couldn't tap into the sewer line. The figures for building a restaurant with all sorts of grease traps, septic tanks, and other required plumbing were astronomical, and we couldn't have afforded the rent even if the man had built the building. We decided that since Billy had experience in building, we would build a new restaurant on the lot that housed the original little green-frame building. Of course, the old building had to be torn down, and we were saddened to do it.

Billy worked at the railroad from 7 a.m. until 3 p.m., and then he would work at the cafe site until 9:30 or 10:00 every night. About the time Billy got the footings dug, it started raining. The first three months of 1980, it rained and rained. Finally the weather cleared enough to have the foundation poured and the block laid for the walls—then came more rain. Because of the weather, it took seven months to complete the building, install all the equipment, and get ready to open.

When we opened the "new" Irondale Cafe on July 22, 1980, we could seat 100 people, and we had a private room to use for overflow and private meetings or parties. There was a small office for me, and the kitchen was quite adequate. We had an automatic dishwasher, two stoves, five deep fryers, and plenty of room to work.

Miss Bess and nephew in the 1950s. Photo courtesy of Mike Fortenberry.

Most of our regular customers were watching and ready for us to open, but I remember two who didn't come back, even though they had regularly visited the back room in our old place. Although segregation had ended quite some time before we bought the original building in 1972, the back room was where black folks liked to sit, enjoy a hamburger or barbecue and beer, and play the Rockola. The two customers I particularly remembered were elderly black men who dropped by the cafe one at a time, usually sometime during the morning, for a beer. They never stayed long—by the time the waitress would get back with their change, they would be ready to go. They didn't come to our new building—it probably didn't give them the privacy they had enjoyed in the old place. We really missed them.

Other than those two gentlemen, our business was back to normal in no time, although in the restaurant business there are very few days when things are completely normal. For instance, a few weeks after we opened our new building, one of the officials from the railroad Billy worked for called me about 9:30 in the morning and asked if he could pick up 50 box lunches by 11:00 a.m. There had been a derailment, and he needed to feed the cleanup crew. We had plenty of sandwich food but not enough desserts. We didn't have time to make another cobbler, so I called the Pizitz store at Eastwood Mall and ordered several cakes. Since I didn't have anyone to cashier for me, I asked a young employee to pick up the cakes for me. He didn't have a car that day, and I told him to take mine.

It seemed to take a long time for him to get back with the cakes, and I started getting nervous—I needed time to slice the cakes and wrap the pieces for the 11 o'clock lunch order. The first thing he said when he arrived back at the cafe was, "Mrs. Mc, I won't ever drive your car again!" He was so upset that I thought he had wrecked my car. He hastily told me what had happened. As he drove into a parking space at the mall, an Irondale police car drove up alongside, and before he could open the door, the policeman was at the window demanding, "What are you doing in Mrs. Mc's car?" He explained that I had sent him to buy cakes and showed the officer my check made out to Pizitz to pay for them. I was very impressed with the Irondale Police Department! The few times I have needed them—and at least once when I didn't, they were right there.

The Word Spreads

A number of newspaper articles reported our progress through the years and brought in new customers, but none as much as Dennis Washburn's article in *The Birmingham News* on March 31, 1979. People poured in after that article was printed and I don't know how we managed to feed them all, but we did! A great deal of our success has been due to "word of mouth" advertising. One morning a regular customer had to stand in line for a few minutes because the restaurant was crowded. As he approached the counter, I passed by him on my way to put out more silverware. He stopped me and said, "Mrs. Mc, I've told at least one hundred people about this place, and I'm not telling anyone else!"

One Monday morning, a customer came in and said, "Mrs. Mc, I've got the funniest story to tell you. Yesterday my daughter was teaching a Sunday School class of four- and five-year-olds. The lesson was about Heaven, and she thought she had the children's attention. After the lesson was over, she asked questions to see how much the children had absorbed. When she asked who could tell her where boys and girls get to go if they're good, one boy raised his hand and said, 'I get to go to IRONDALE CAFE!'

I wish I had that little boy's answer on tape! It beats any advertisement any of the fast-food places have come up with. Needless to say, that little boy was one of our favorites! We knew his mother and father and brother, too, and the whole family was special even before that happened.

We have watched a lot of children grow up at the Irondale Cafe, and it does our hearts good to know we have had a small part in their lives. One young man who still comes in with his family has eaten with us since he was about eight years old. He always came through the line at Sunday noon asking for two servings of corn and one of peas. At Christmas time one year, we were closed both the Sunday before and the Sunday after Christmas. The first Sunday we were open again, he came through the line and said, "I want two servings of corn and two servings of peas!" When his mother said, "My, you're hungry today," he replied, "Well, I haven't had any for two weeks!"

Bursting at the Seams—Again!

When we first moved into the new building, we were open for business seven days a week. We served three meals daily Monday through Saturday and lunch on Sunday. We had planned to close one day a week, but we were checking to see which would be the best day. We knew we would develop a good Sunday business, but we weren't sure about Saturday or Monday.

After several months, we dropped Saturdays. Some people don't understand that, but since we are not on the "main drag," so to speak, business on Saturdays was never consistent. After four years, we decided to close at night, too. We were losing money staying open after 5 p.m., and with the great lunch business we had through the week and on Sundays, we decided it was foolish to continue to stay open late. Even after we started closing at night, we continued to grow, and by the beginning of 1990, we had outgrown our "new" building.

In December 1990, the building next door, the old Daly Hardware Store, came up for sale. The real estate agent came into the cafe and asked if I was interested in buying the building. Of course, I knew we needed the building, but I told him I would have to talk with Billy. We agreed we could use the extra space, and we signed a contract and gave him a check for the earnest money a few days later. When we got home that day, Billy turned to me and said, "Honey, do you think we did the right thing?"

I said, "Now you ask me—after we've put our money up! It's like the situation we were in back in 1979 when we either had to put up or shut up. Now we've either got to expand or back away from business, and I didn't learn that while I was struggling to build the business." We laughed and went to bed knowing two things: We needed more room and we would do everything we could to be successful.

Fried Green Tomatoes Galore

In January 1992, the movie *Fried Green Tomatoes* hit the screen. It premiered at the Cobb Galleria Theatre in Birmingham, and Fannie Flagg, Bess Fortenberry's niece and author of the book, came with a lot of her friends and associates. She left tickets for us at the box office. All of our family except Connie, who was in graduate school at the University of Tennessee in Knoxville, went to see it. A couple of friends and three of our employees, including Virginia Johnson, came with us. Ms. Flagg always made Virginia feel special. Virginia had worked for Ms. Flagg's Aunt Bess and still works for us. She is special.

The movie enthralled us—it was like knowing Miss Bess when she was younger. It was such a wonderful, sweet, hilarious, and touching movie that I think everyone who saw it once went back to see it again.

The Irondale depot in the 1930s.

We couldn't have imagined the huge impact the movie would have on our business. Right after it opened, tourists from all over started coming to the "Whistle Stop" Cafe. On February 5, 1992, *The Birmingham News* ran an article with a picture of two of my cooks holding a peck basket of green tomatoes. The caption read "Seen the movie? Now taste the title."

Everyone who comes to the cafe for the first time wants to know all about Miss Bess and our restaurant—and almost all the customers, new and old, order fried green tomatoes! During the past three years, we have not opened for lunch or dinner without fried green tomatoes. We fry 60 or 70 pounds every weekday and more than that on Sundays. It's almost a miracle that we've been able to do it. The people at the Finley Avenue Produce Market have been more than helpful in keeping us supplied with all the green tomatoes we need.

When we started frying so many tomatoes, we knew we had to have a batter mix that would be good to use in a deep fryer. We experimented, and my husband came up with the one we are using now. We've found that it's also very good with any vegetable you want to fry that calls for a liquid batter. People have told us they use it for onion rings, eggplant, mushrooms, squash, zucchini, and even corn dogs.

You can buy our Irondale Cafe Original Whistlestop™ Recipes Brand Fried Green Tomato Batter Mix as well as our batter mixes for seafood and chicken and a delicious cobbler mix. The mixes are available in several states in local grocery stores—not to mention Juliette, Georgia, where the movie was filmed—and will soon be available in your area.

We've been the owners of the Irondale Cafe for 22 years now, and looking back, I wonder what would have happened if Miss Bess Fortenberry had sold the cafe to the other couple who wanted to buy it. I'm very sure of one thing: If someone had told me back then how hard I would work in the years to come, I never would have believed it! When you have the responsibility of a business, you get up and go to work even if you feel bad. For some 15 years, I was at the cafe every day it was open.

We are really thankful for our business. We worked hard and long and had a good business before *Fried Green Tomatoes,* and now we are continuing to grow. No matter how many customers we get, though, we will still try our best to give everyone the same good service, the same good food, and the same friendliness that we did before the movie.

Fannie Flagg has been so kind to us and mentions us quite often in interviews. We consider her a very good friend and one of the family. Part of the reason I've written this book is that she encouraged me to write it. All of us here at the Irondale Cafe, the "Original Whistle Stop" and home of Fried Green Tomatoes, hope you enjoy sharing our history and recipes with your family and friends.

CHAPTER 2

Timesaving Tips for "Working" Homemakers

Life is not a wanting and a getting,
but a being and a becoming.

— MATTHEW ARNOLD —

Timesaving Tips

There are many things that can help today's "working" homemakers save time and yet cook delicious meals. Instead of being a dreaded task, cooking can be an exciting time of the day. Irondale Cafe is known for its "home cooking," and I want to share with you some of the things I have learned from operating the cafe, my "home" for the past 22 years.

One of the most important things in cooking is "prep work." By carefully planning meals and preparing many of the items ahead, you can save time in the long run. Plan daily menus for a week at a time, and prepare a shopping list for foods needed for those menus. Not only will this help you shop and prepare meals more efficiently, but it will also help your family members. They will be able to plan their lunches around the family meals, making sure they don't eat the same thing twice in a day, and that they do eat a balanced daily diet to get all the nutrition they need.

Of course there will be times when you'll want or have to stop for dinner or take-out food somewhere—like the Irondale Cafe. For the most part, though, it will save you time to use your scheduled daily menus and prep some of the foods ahead of time. Prep work can be done in the evening after supper. Most of today's husbands pitch in and help, and it can be a time of togetherness for a couple. If you have a television in your kitchen, you can keep up with programs you like to watch while you're working. You will really appreciate the prep work you've done when you come in the next evening and get dinner on the stove in a matter of minutes.

Prepping Vegetables

Peel and chop onions, dice bell peppers and celery, and peel and cut up carrots to cook later as a vegetable or to add to stews and soups. Store the prepped vegetables in airtight containers or plastic bags for up to three days in the refrigerator.

If you have potato salad or mashed potatoes on your menu, peel and wash the potatoes, and put them in airtight containers, covering them with cold water. If you are making potato salad, you can go ahead and dice the potatoes. It's not necessary to dice them for mashed potatoes. Whole potatoes cook quickly and can be mashed and then whipped with butter or margarine and milk with your mixer. Not dicing potatoes for mashed potatoes will save you time.

Squash can be washed, cut up, and refrigerated for a day or two. Pole beans can be snapped and strung ahead of time and then washed and refrigerated. Any fresh vegetable you plan to cook can be prepped a day or two ahead and refrigerated.

Sweet Potatoes

When you plan to make sweet potato soufflé, candied yams, or sweet potato pie, wash the sweet potatoes in cold water, pull off any strings, put the potatoes in a large saucepan, and cover with water. Bring the water to a boil, and cook over medium-high heat until a knife easily penetrates the skin. (Be careful not to overcook or the potatoes will get too soft and be hard to handle.) Pour off the water, and let the potatoes cool either in a colander or in the pan. Peel or pull off the skin, and refrigerate the potatoes in an airtight container for a day or two. It isn't recommended that you wash the potatoes after peeling or let them stand in water; just put them in a colander until all of them are peeled. If you are planning to make candied yams, you can cut the potatoes into pieces before refrigerating them.

Macaroni and Cheese

A day or two ahead, cook the macaroni according to the package directions, drain it in a colander, and rinse it thoroughly with cold water. Put the well-drained macaroni into an airtight container, and refrigerate it. It's a good idea to buy grated cheese for making macaroni and cheese recipes—it saves time, and it's not much more expensive. With the macaroni cooked ahead, it only takes 5 or 10 minutes to combine the ingredients and have the dish ready for the oven.

Meat Loaf

If you are planning to cook meat loaf, you will be amazed at the time it saves if you dice the onions and bell peppers ahead of time (store them in airtight containers in the refrigerator). If you buy family-pack ground chuck, you can mix enough meat loaf for two meals and freeze one loaf (wrap it first in heavy-duty wax paper and then in aluminum foil, or use a heavy-duty plastic bag). You can also take part of the ground chuck and cook it in a skillet, stirring until done and draining it in a colander set in a large bowl or pan (to catch the grease rather than letting it run into your sink). The cooked meat can be divided into several bags and used in the next day or two to make spaghetti sauce, tacos, taco salad, or even homemade pizza. If you cook a large quantity of meat, place it in heavy-duty plastic bags, and freeze it; it doesn't take long to thaw.

Rice

Rice is another thing that can be cooked ahead, even though it doesn't take long to cook. If you plan to have two rice meals in the same week, cook enough rice for both recipes. After you have taken out what you need for the first recipe, pour the remainder into a colander, and rinse with cold water. (When rice is rinsed with cold water immediately after cooking, it will stay fluffy and won't get gummy.) Refrigerate the extra rice in an airtight container for a day or two. When you are ready to use it, the rice is ready to mix with the other ingredients of the recipe; if you are planning to serve the cooked rice with gravy or a meat, place it in a colander, and run hot water over it.

Dried Beans

Take out the amount of beans you want to cook, and either tie up the bag or pour the remaining beans into a jar or canister for storing (be sure to put the bag in the jar so you have the directions when you cook the beans later). Pour the beans onto a plate, and look over them. Discard little pieces of beans that have a hole in them and any tiny rocks or pieces of dirt. Put the "looked over" beans into a container until you are ready to cook them. About an hour before you are ready to cook them, place the beans in a boiler, and cover them with very hot water. Let them stand about 40 minutes, adding more hot water as the water is absorbed; while the beans are soaking, fill another boiler with water, add 1 teaspoon of salt and the other seasonings, and bring the water to a boil. Drain the beans in a colander, rinse with hot water (never use cold water on beans that have been soaking in hot water), and add them to the pot of boiling water.

Getting Ready for Thanksgiving and Christmas

As the holidays near and your thoughts turn to turkey and dressing, use these tips to make preparing the special meals quicker and easier.

A couple of weeks before Thanksgiving or Christmas, before you really get busy, buy the ingredients for cornbread and biscuits. Take one day at home, and bake a large batch of cornbread and biscuits. Let the cornbread cool, and then crumble and freeze it in a heavy-duty plastic bag (be sure bread is cool before you put it in freezer so it won't sweat). Do the same with the biscuits. White breadcrumbs are often used, but we've found that biscuits make the best dressing.

Two or three days before you are going to make your dressing, peel and wash the onions and celery. Then cut them up, and refrigerate them in an airtight container. You might want to use our recipe for Baked Turkey with Traditional Southern Cornbread Dressing (page 46).

HINTS

Idaho or russet potatoes are best for baking, mashing, and creamy potato salad. Red cobbler potatoes are best for stewed potatoes, stews, and chunky potato salad. Cobbler potatoes do not cook to pieces like baking potatoes.

1 tablespoon cornstarch is equal to 2 tablespoons flour when thickening gravies, soups, and sauces. When adding cornstarch to hot liquids, mix it first with a small amount of cold water, blending well, and then add it to the hot liquid, stirring constantly.

1 cup sifted all-purpose flour is equal to 1 cup plus 2 tablespoons sifted cake flour.

1 (1-ounce) square chocolate is equal to 3 tablespoons cocoa plus 1 tablespoon butter.

1 teaspoon baking powder is equal to 1 teaspoon baking soda plus ½ teaspoon cream of tartar.

1 cup milk is equal to ½ cup evaporated milk plus ½ cup water.

1 cup sour milk is equal to 1 cup sweet milk mixed with 1 tablespoon vinegar or lemon juice.

COOKING TERMS

BASTE: To moisten with liquid during cooking, using a spoon or brush.

BIND: To thicken the liquid of a soup, gravy, or stew with a starch, such as flour or cornstarch, or with egg yolks.

BLANCH: To place in boiling water for a given amount of time and then in cold water, to partially cook or peel a food.

BRAISE: To sear or brown in fat, then cook slowly, covered with a minimum amount of liquid, on the stove or in the oven.

BREADING: A coating of flour and/or breadcrumbs used on foods that are to be fried. Foods may be dipped into beaten egg or milk to help the coating stick.

JULIENNE: Food is cut into very thin, long strips.

KNEAD: To work dough by pushing it with the heel of your hand, folding it over and pushing over again until it has reached the degree of smoothness indicated in recipe.

MARINATE: To soak food, usually meat or fish, in a liquid that will add to flavor or make the food more tender.

SUBSTITUTIONS

1 teaspoon allspice =	½ teaspoon cinnamon + ⅛ teaspoon cloves + ¼ teaspoon nutmeg
1 square baking chocolate =	3 tablespoons cocoa + 1 tablespoon butter
1 teaspoon baking powder =	¼ teaspoon soda + ½ teaspoon cream of tartar
1 cup brown sugar =	1 scant cup white sugar + 1 teaspoon molasses
1 tablespoon cornstarch =	2 tablespoons flour or 4 teaspoons quick-cooking tapioca
1 cup self-rising flour =	1 cup flour + 1 teaspoon baking powder + ½ teaspoon baking soda + ½ teaspoon salt
1 tablespoon fresh herbs =	1 teaspoon dried herbs
1 teaspoon dry mustard =	1 tablespoon prepared mustard
1 teaspoon poultry seasoning =	¼ teaspoon thyme + ¾ teaspoon sage
1 teaspoon pumpkin pie spices =	½ teaspoon ginger + ½ teaspoon cinnamon + ½ teaspoon allspice + ½ teaspoon nutmeg
1 cup buttermilk =	1 cup sweet milk + 1 tablespoon vinegar or lemon juice OR 1 cup plain yogurt
1 cup ketchup =	1 cup tomato sauce + ½ cup sugar + 2 tablespoons vinegar
1 cup chili sauce =	1 cup tomato sauce + ½ cup sugar + 2 tablespoon vinegar + 2 teaspoons chili powder
1 clove garlic =	½ teaspoon garlic powder + ⅛ teaspoon instant garlic flakes
1 cup honey =	¾ cup sugar + ¼ cup liquid
1 medium lemon =	2 -3 tablespoons lemon juice
1 cup milk =	½ cup evaporated milk + ½ cup water OR 4 tablespoons powdered milk + 1 cup water
1 cup molasses =	¾ cup water or honey + ¼ cup dark brown sugar

1 medium onion =	2 tablespoons instant onion OR 1½ teaspoons onion powder
1 cup sour cream =	1 cup evaporated milk + 1 tablespoon vinegar OR 1 cup heavy cream + 1 tablespoon vinegar OR ⅞ cup buttermilk + 3 tablespoons butter
1 cup tomato juice =	½ cup tomato sauce + ½ cup water
1 cup whipping cream =	¾ cup whole milk + ⅓ cup butter
1 cake compressed yeast =	1 package or 2 teaspoons active dry yeast

We could never learn to be brave and patient, if there were only joy in the world.

— HELEN KELLER —

EQUIVALENTS

Green beans, 1 pound = 3 cups, uncooked

Beans, dried, ½ pound = 1 cup, uncooked

Bread, 2 slices = 1 cup crumbs

Butter, 1 stick = ½ cup or 8 table-spoons

Carrots, 6 to 9, 1 pound = 2 cups, cooked

Cocoa, 1 pound = 4 cups

Coffee, 1 pound, 5 cups = 40 to 50 cups perked

Cheese, 1 pound = 4 cups, grated

Cream cheese, 3 ounces = 6 tablespoons

Dates, pitted, 1 pound = 2 cups

Eggs, 1 = ¼ cup

Flour, sifted, 1 pound = 4 cups

Flour, cake, 1 pound = 4 ½ - 5 cups

Graham cracker crumbs 11 crackers, crushed = 1 cup

Lemon, 1 juice = 2½ tablespoons

Macaroni, 1 cup uncooked = 2 cups cooked

Marshmallows, ¼ pound = 16

Milk, condensed, 14 ounces = 1¼ cups

Milk, evaporated, 6 ounces = ⅔ cup, 14½ ounces = 1⅔ cups

Noodles, 1 cup uncooked = 1½ cup cooked

Nuts, shelled, ½ pound = 2 cups chopped

Peas, in pod, 1 pound = 1 - 1½ cups shelled

Potatoes, 1 pound = 2 - 5 medium or 2 -3 cups cooked and mashed

Prunes, 1 pound = 4 cups cooked

Raisins, 1 pound = 3 cups

Rice, uncooked, 1 pound = 2¼ cups

Rice, uncooked,1 cup = 3 cups cooked

Sugar, 1 pound = 2 cups

Sugar, brown, 1 pound = 2¼ cups

Sugar, powdered, 1 pound = 3½ cups

Tea, loose, 1 pound = 5 cups, 155 cups brewed

Whipping cream, ½ pint = 2 cups whipped

PAN SIZES

Tube pans:

7½ x 3-inch Bundt = 6 cups

9 x 3½-inch tube = 9 cups

9 x 3½-inch angel cake = 12 cups

10 x 4-inch angel cake pan = 18 cups

HERBS AND SPICES FOR SEASONING

Allspice: sweet potatoes, squash, fruit, pickles, pot roast, fish, eggs

Basil: green or vegetable salad, potatoes, tomatoes, carrots, spinach, eggplant, peas, cheese, eggs, jelly, noodles, rice, veal, fish, meatloaf, beef stew, duck, pork

Bay Leaf: soups, stews, chowders, marinades, pickles, fish, variety of meats

Caraway Seeds: beets, cabbage, carrots, cauliflower, green beans, potatoes, sauerkraut, turnips, zucchini, meat marinade, cake, cookies, rice, rye bread, goose, ribs, beef, lamb stew, pork

Cardamom: sweet potatoes, squash, pickles, fruit, soups, grape jelly

Celery Seed: vegetables, tomatoes, potato and fruit salads, pickles, stuffing, egg dishes, stews, soups, meat loaf

Chili Powder: corn, eggplant, bean casseroles, tomato or barbecue sauces, dips, egg dishes, cheese, chicken, stews, meat loaf, marinades

Cinnamon: carrots, beets, sweet potatoes, baked goods, pickles, chicken, beef stew, lamb, ham, pork

Cloves: carrots, beets, sweet potatoes, tomatoes, fruit, baked products, fish, stuffing, pot roast, beef

Curry Powder: dried beans, fruit, dips, breads, marinades, beef, chicken, lamb, meatballs, pork, veal, eggs

Dill Seed: salads, sauerkraut, green beans, pickles, beets, breads, egg dishes, stews, fish, chicken

Fennel Seed: vegetables, baked and stewed apples, pickles, sauerkraut, breads, cakes, cookies, cheese, egg dishes, fish, stews, marinades

Garlic: salads, dressings, tomato dishes, dill pickles, soups, dips, sauces, stews, bread, meat, poultry, fish, marinades

Ginger: vegetables, baked or stewed fruits, pickles, baked products, fish, poultry, all meats, soups, beverages, Oriental dishes

Mace: vegetables, jellies, pickles, breads, baked products, fruits, poultry, fish, meat loaf, chowder

Marjoram: broccoli, carrots, cauliflower, peas, spinach, squash, tomato dishes, mushrooms, pizza, spaghetti, egg dishes, breads, soups, meats, fish, poultry

Mint: tea, punches, jelly, sherbet, vegetables, sauces, lamb

Dry Mustard: salad dressing, vegetables, egg and cheese dishes, meat, poultry

Mustard Seed: potato salad, pickles, coleslaw, cabbage, sauerkraut, corned beef

Nutmeg: baked goods, hot beverages, puddings, salads, vegetables, fruits, seafood, eggs, poultry, pickles

Onion Powder: dips, soups, stews, all meats, fish, poultry, salads, vegetables, stuffing, cheese and egg dishes, breads, rice dishes

Oregano: tomatoes, pasta sauces, pizza, chili, barbecue sauce, vegetable soup, egg and cheese dishes, onions, stuffing, meat, poultry, fish

Parsley: tomato and meat sauces, soups, coleslaw, breads, stuffing, broiled or fried fish, poultry

Black Pepper: pickles, vegetables, fish, meat, poultry, eggs, gravies

Cayenne Pepper: vegetables, pickles, soups, cheese dishes, sauces, pizza, eggs, curried dishes, dips, tamale pie, fish, poultry, meat

White Pepper: white or light-colored meats, vegetables, mashed potatoes, white sauces and gravies

Lemon Pepper: chicken, fish, seafood

Poppy Seed: fruit salad dressings, compotes, breads, pie crust, cookies, cakes, cheese sticks, scrambled eggs, noodles

Poultry Seasoning: stuffing, soup, meatloaf

Rosemary: cauliflower, potatoes, spinach, mushrooms, turnips, fruits, marinades, soups, stews, poultry, fish, meats

Saffron: rice, curries, baked goods, chicken, seafood

Sage: stuffing, eggplant, lima beans, onions, potatoes, tomatoes, cheese sauces, soups, chowders, poultry, fish, meats

Sesame Seed: salads, vegetables, noodles, soups, canapés, breads, cookies, casseroles, dips, stuffing, pie crust and fillings, cakes

Tarragon: casseroles, sour cream sauces, marinades, egg dishes, pot roasts, meats, fish, poultry

Thyme: meat, poultry, fish, vegetables

Turmeric: rice dishes, curried meats, fish, poultry, egg dishes, pickles, cakes, breads

Vanilla: baked goods, puddings, beverages

One enemy is too many,
and a hundred friends too few.

— GERMAN PROVERB —

CHAPTER 3

What's for Supper?

Meats and Fish

One-Pan Meals

Home-Cooked Vegetables-Southern Style

Salads

Meats and Fish

No one is useless in this world
who lightens the burden of anyone else.

— Charles Dickens —

Beef Tips and Rice

- 1 (3-pound) very lean sirloin tip roast, cut into small pieces
- 1 quart water
- 1 medium onion, finely chopped
- 1 bell pepper, finely chopped
- 1/4 cup Worcestershire sauce
- 1/4 cup soy sauce
- 1 teaspoon garlic powder
- 1 teaspoon seasoned salt
- 1 teaspoon black pepper
- 2 tablespoons self-rising flour
- 1 cup water
- 8 cups cooked rice

Combine cubed beef, 1 quart water, onion, bell pepper, Worcestershire sauce, and soy sauce in a Dutch oven. Place over medium-high heat and bring to a boil. Add garlic powder, seasoned salt, and black pepper. Reduce heat, and simmer for about 1 hour.

Mix self-rising flour and 1 cup water, and stir into hot mixture. Cook over medium heat until thickened.

Serve over cooked rice.

Yield: 10-12 servings

Beef Stew

- 2 pounds lean stewing beef, cut into 1-inch cubes
- 1 teaspoon salt
- 1 teaspoon garlic powder
- 1 teaspoon seasoned salt
- 1 teaspoon black pepper
- 3 or 4 large potatoes, cubed (large red cobbler potatoes work best)
- 3 large onions, quartered
- 2 (14 1/2-ounce) cans whole or diced tomatoes, undrained
- 2 (15 1/2-ounce) cans tomato sauce

Rinse stew meat, and place in large boiler; add spices and water to cover. Bring to boil, and reduce heat to simmer. Cook for 1 hour or until meat is tender (be sure to keep beef covered with water during cooking).

Cook potatoes and onions in water. When potatoes, and onions are tender, drain in colander and combine in large pot with meat. Add tomatoes and tomato sauce, stirring well. Simmer 25 to 30 minutes.

Note: You can cook 8-10 carrots peeled and cut into 1-inch pieces, with potatoes and onions, if desired.

Yield: 10-12 servings

Brunswick Stew

- 1 (5-pound) stewing hen
- 1 (3-pound) chuck roast, cooked, cooled, and shredded
- 1 (3-pound) pork loin roast cooked, cooled, and shredded
- 5 cups beef broth
- 3 (16-ounce) cans diced tomatoes, undrained
- 2 (12-ounce) cans whole-kernel corn, drained
- 1 (15-ounce) can tomato sauce
- 3 large onions, chopped finely
- 1½ cups ketchup
- ½ cup vinegar
- ⅓ cup Worcestershire sauce
- 1 tablespoon salt
- 2 teaspoons pepper
- 2 teaspoons hot sauce
- 1 teaspoon garlic salt
- 1 teaspoon lemon juice

Place chicken in a large Dutch oven or pot; add water to cover. Bring to a boil; cover and simmer 2 hours or until tender. Remove chicken from broth and let cool; remove meat from bones, and chop into fine pieces. Transfer 5 cups chicken broth to a large stockpot; reserve remaining broth for use in other recipes (broth may be frozen). Add chopped chicken and remaining ingredients, stirring well. Bring to a boil, reduce heat, and simmer, uncovered for 3 hours.

Yield: 1½ gallons

Creamed Chicken

- 1/4 cup butter or margarine
- 1/4 cup self-rising flour
- 1 1/2 cups milk
- 1/2 teaspoon salt
- dash of cayenne pepper
- dash of black pepper
- 2 cups diced cooked chicken
- 3 large biscuits or 6 slices toast (dry)

Melt margarine in a large skillet over low heat; add flour, stirring until smooth. Cook 1 to 2 minutes, stirring constantly. Gradually add milk; cook over medium heat, stirring constantly until mixture thickens. Stir in salt and peppers and add chicken; simmer until chicken is heated thoroughly. If mixture is too thick, add a small amount of water, stirring well. Serve over open biscuits or toast.

Note: 1/2 cup thinly sliced sauteed celery adds a delicious taste to this dish.

Yield: 6 servings

Take time to laugh; it is the music of the soul.

— ANONYMOUS —

The Best Fried Chicken

When you buy fresh chicken to fry, I recommend immediately skinning and rinsing it well. Place the chicken in an airtight container with water, some ice, and salt. (The amount of salt depends on the amount of chicken. For 5 or 6 pieces, use 1 teaspoon of salt dissolved in the water. Be careful not to get too much or the chicken will be too salty.)

When we prepare our chicken this way at the Irondale Cafe, we never add extra salt. Store the chicken in the refrigerator for up to two days; drain the water, and pour buttermilk over the chicken. Return it to the refrigerator until you are ready to fry it.

Sift 2 to 3 cups self-rising flour into a large mixing bowl; set aside.

Remove cleaned and skinned chicken from refrigerator. Remove from the buttermilk and place on platter; let excess buttermilk drain off. Place drained chicken into flour, turning to coat well, patting it on if necessary.

Heat oil in frying pan or fryer to approximately 350°. Place pieces of chicken in pan (I place chicken breasts with the thick side down, bone turned toward center of pan). You may have to turn the heat down some, but remember that the cold chicken will cool the oil, and if the oil is not hot enough, the chicken will absorb the oil and be soggy.

Fry at medium-high heat approximately 7 minutes; turn chicken over, and brown other side for 6 to 7 minutes. (Be sure the chicken is well done. I fry dark meat as long as white meat because of the larger bones in the leg and thigh.)

Note: You may cover the chicken and let it steam for a few minutes, but for crispier chicken, leave it uncovered.

Note: For spicier chicken, I recommend using Irondale Cafe Original Whistlestop™ Recipes Brand Fried Chicken Batter Mix.

Chicken and Dumplings

2½ to 3 pounds broiler-fryer, cut up and skinned
1 tablespoon salt
1 teaspoon pepper
¾ cup milk
½ cup margarine
Plain Pastry, chilled

Place chicken in a saucepan and cover with water; add salt and pepper, and bring to a boil. Cover, reduce heat, and simmer 45 minutes to 1 hour or until chicken is very tender. Remove chicken from broth, and let cool. Bone chicken, and cut into small pieces.

Place chilled pastry on a lightly floured surface and roll thin. Cut into 3-inch strips. Bring broth to a boil, and add milk and margarine. Drop pastry strips into boiling broth; reduce heat, and cook 15 minutes. Keep adding pastry, stirring often to keep the strips from sticking together. Cover and cook 6 to 8 minutes longer; uncover and add diced chicken. Cook until thoroughly heated.

Note: If broth has not thickened, blend 1 tablespoon self-rising flour and ½ cup water, and add to broth, stirring well. Cook over medium heat 5 to 10 minutes until mixture thickens.

Yield: 6-8 servings

Plain Pastry

Use for Chicken and Dumplings and Chicken Potpie.

2 cups all-purpose flour
1 teaspoon salt
⅔ cup shortening
5 to 6 tablespoons cold water

Sift together flour and salt; cut in shortening with pastry blender until mixture is crumbly. Add cold water a little at a time, tossing with a fork until all the flour coated bits of shortening are dampened. Turn mixture out onto a square of wax paper or form a ball by pressing firmly. Chill pastry for easier handling.

Yield: 1 dumplings recipe; 1 large or 2 medium potpies

Chicken Potpie

1 (2½ to 3-pound) broiler-fryer, cut up and skinned
1 tablespoon salt
1 teaspoon pepper
1 (16-ounce) bag frozen mixed vegetables
1 small jar diced pimento
2 tablespoons self-rising flour
1½ cups water
Plain Pastry, chilled
1 stick margarine, melted

Place chicken in a saucepan, and cover with water; add salt and pepper, bring to a boil. Cover, reduce heat, and simmer 45 minutes to 1 hour or until chicken is very tender. Remove chicken from broth and let cool. Bone chicken, and cut into small pieces.

Cook frozen mixed vegetables until tender; drain. Add pimento, and mix well.

Reheat broth, add vegetable mixture and diced chicken. Combine flour and water, and blend well; stir into broth mixture and cook over medium heat until slightly thickened. Set aside.

Place chilled pastry on a lightly floured surface, and roll thin; cut into ½-inch strips. Place strips of pastry side by side, ⅛ inch apart in a large baking dish; top with broth mixture. Place additional pastry strips very close together over the top of broth mixture. Brush with melted margarine, and bake at 350° for 30 to 40 minutes or until top is golden brown.

Serve hot.

Yield: 6-8 servings

Chicken Cordon Bleu

6 chicken breast fillets
1 cup sour cream
6 slices American cheese
6 (1-ounce) slices cooked ham
6 slices bacon
1 (10-ounce) can cream of mushroom soup
hot cooked white rice

Rinse chicken fillets and pat dry. Brush one side of each fillet with sour cream, and top with a slice of cheese and ham. Roll up fillet to enclose filling; wrap with bacon, and secure with wooden pick. Place in baking dish; bake at 350° for 1 hour. Pour soup over chicken; bake an additional 15 minutes or until chicken is tender. Serve with hot rice.

Yield: 6 servings

Smothered Chicken

½ cup self-rising flour
½ teaspoon salt
½ teaspoon pepper
1 (2½ to 3-pound) broiler-fryer, cut up
¼ cup butter or margarine
½ cup oil
1 tablespoon self-rising flour
1 cup Half & Half
salt and pepper to taste
biscuits, potatoes, or hot cooked white rice

Combine flour, salt, and pepper. Dredge chicken in flour mixture, coating well. Melt butter or margarine in large skillet and brown chicken. Cover, reduce heat, and simmer about 20 minutes. Move chicken to platter, reserving cooking liquid.

Combine 1 tablespoon flour and Half & Half, stirring until blended; pour into reserved cooking liquid, and cook over medium heat until mixture starts to thicken. Stir in salt and pepper to taste; return chicken to skillet and cover. Simmer 10 minutes, adding a small amount of water if needed. Serve with biscuits, potatoes, or cooked rice.

Yield: 6-8 servings

Great Homemade Chili

2 pounds extra-lean ground chuck
2 medium onions, chopped
2 cloves garlic, minced
2 tablespoons margarine
3 cups water
1 (14½-ounce) can diced tomatoes, undrained
1 (15-ounce) can tomato sauce
2 teaspoons salt
1 teaspoon sugar
⅓ cup chili powder
½ teaspoon cayenne pepper
2 quarts pinto beans in broth (or 4 [15-ounce] cans undrained)
1 (1-ounce) bar unsweetened chocolate (optional)
½ cup strong black coffee (optional)
⅓ cup uncooked oats
saltines or cornbread

Cook beef until almost done, scrambling with a fork; pour into colander to drain. Rinse skillet well with very hot water to remove all fat. Saute onions and garlic in margarine.

Place cooked beef into a large boiler or Dutch oven; add sauteed onions and garlic, water, tomatoes, and tomato sauce. Cook over medium heat until almost boiling; reduce heat to medium-high. Add salt, sugar, chili powder, cayenne pepper, and pinto beans, and stir well. When mixture again reaches boiling point, drop in chocolate, stirring so chocolate will melt. Add coffee, and stir well. Sprinkle dry oats into mixture, stirring so oats don't lump. Simmer for 1 hour. If mixture is thin, increase heat, and boil 5 to 10 minutes, stirring constantly to keep mixture from sticking.

Note: Serve hot with saltines or cornbread.

Note: Sprinkle shredded cheese on top as an extra bonus.

Yield: 6-8 servings

Baked Fresh Ham

Using a sharp knife, trim off skin and fat, leaving only a small amount of fat on the ham; set skin and fat aside. Lightly sprinkle ham with salt and pepper. Wrap in heavy-duty aluminum foil, and bake at 350° for 3½ to 4 hours.

Let ham cool; slice or pull meat off bone. The cooked meat can be used in several ways. It's good with dressing you can make with the drippings or barbecue sauce. It's also good in sandwiches with mayonnaise, mustard, or barbecue sauce.

To make cracklings, use a sharp knife to cut the fat away from the skin in large strips, if possible. Cut fat into ½-inch cubes, and place them into a saucepan over medium heat. Let the fat cubes cook until they are golden brown, stirring every few minutes to keep them separated. Drain into a colander placed in a pan. (The cooled drippings, called lard, can be used for cooking. We usually stay away from this type of shortening because of the fat, but some people still use it.)

Let the cracklings drain well. To make Southern Cracklin' Bread, stir some cracklings into your favorite cornbread recipe; you might want to cut the amount of shortening by one-third because the cracklings will add fat to the batter.

To make meat skins, place the skin on a cutting board. Use a sharp knife to cut the skin into strips 3 or 4 inches long. Place strips in a shallow pan, and bake at 300° to 325° until skins curl up and brown. Stand skins against sides of colander to drain. Sprinkle salt on them while they are hot.

Wealth consists not in having great possessions, but in having few wants.

— EPICURUS —

Country Ham and Red-eye Gravy

- 1/4 inch thick slices country ham, 1 per serving
- 1 cup coffee
- 1 teaspoon sugar

Trim rind off ham slices, and discard rind. Cut off extra fat, but do not discard; leave small amount of fat around edge. Place ham slices and trimmed fat into a skillet.

Cook over medium heat 10 minutes, turning several times. Place ham slices on a platter, and keep warm in a 200° oven. Add coffee and sugar to drippings in skillet. Cook over medium heat for a few minutes; increase heat, and boil until gravy thickens.

Note: You will not have a lot of gravy, but you won't need much. This is one case where a little goes a long, long way!

Yield: 1 slice per serving

Baked Cured Ham

- 16-20 pound cured ham
- cloves
- 1/2 cup brown sugar
- 1/4 cup Coca-Cola
- maraschino cherries, halved
- pineapple slices

Using a sharp knife, trim off skin and fat, leaving just a thin layer of fat on one side of ham. Score fat, place ham in baking pan, and cover with heavy-duty aluminum foil. Bake at 350° for 1 hour. Reduce heat to 300° to finish baking, allowing 18 to 20 minutes per pound for a whole large ham and 20 to 30 minutes for a half ham. Thirty minutes before ham is done, remove from oven; place whole cloves in the scored fat, and baste with a mixture of brown sugar and Coca-Cola. Bake ham uncovered for final 30 minutes. Decorate baked ham with maraschino cherry halves and pineapple slices.

Note: Trimming the fat gives you a delicious ham that is not greasy.

Yield: 12-16 servings

Liver and Onions

1 pound deveined liver
salt
pepper
1 cup self-rising flour
1/4 cup oil
2 large onions, broken into circles

Sprinkle both sides of each piece of liver with salt and pepper. Sprinkle self-rising flour onto a flat surface; flour liver on both sides. Brown both sides of liver in a large skillet using 1/4 cup oil. Cover liver with onion; simmer, covered, 30 minutes.

Note: If skillet gets dry, add 1/2 cup water.

Yield: 4 servings

Baked Roast

1 (3 to 4-pound) boneless rump or eye-of-round roast
1 1/2 tablespoons Worcestershire sauce
1/2 tablespoon soy sauce (optional)
1 teaspoon pepper
1 teaspoon seasoned salt
1 teaspoon garlic powder
1 teaspoon salt
1 1/2 to 2 cups water
1/4 cup self-rising flour
1 cup water

Rub roast with Worcestershire sauce and soy sauce; sprinkle seasonings over meat. (The seasonings will stick to the meat better if it's rubbed with Worcestershire.) Wrap roast tightly with heavy-duty aluminum foil, and place into baking pan. Pour 1 1/2 to 2 cups water in pan. Bake roast at 350° for 3 to 4 hours. Remove roast from foil, and place roast on platter or cutting board; carefully pour drippings from foil into skillet or saucepan. To make gravy, combine flour and water, and blend well. Pour flour mixture into drippings, and cook over medium heat until thickened, stirring constantly.

Note: Roast can be sliced while warm, but it slices better when cool. If roast is cold, place it in the gravy to serve hot.

Yield: 8-10 servings

Meat Loaf

- 2 eggs, beaten
- 1/3 cup milk
- 1/2 cup tomato sauce
- 1 teaspoon salt
- 1/2 teaspoon garlic powder (optional)
- 1 teaspoon rubbed sage
- 1 1/2 cups white bread or biscuit crumbs
- 2 pounds ground chuck
- 1 cup finely chopped onions
- 1 bell pepper, cored and chopped
- 1/3 cup uncooked oats
- 1 cup diced tomatoes

Combine beaten eggs, milk, and tomato sauce in a large bowl. Add seasonings, and stir well. Add breadcrumbs, and let stand a few minutes until soggy. Add meat, onions, bell pepper, oats, and diced tomatoes; mix well.

Place mixture into loaf pan or Pyrex dish and press out to edges, smoothing with hands. Bake at 375° for 45 minutes to 1 hour or until firm.

Note: After baking for approximately 25 minutes, you may take meat loaf out of oven and drain any fat or dripping off top; return to oven to finish baking.

Yield: 6-8 servings

There are no strangers here,
only friends we have not met.

— ANONYMOUS —

Pork Chops

2 T-bone (center-cut) pork chops for each serving
salt and pepper to taste
2 cups self-rising flour
½ cup vegetable oil
⅓ cup self-rising flour
1½ cups water

Rinse chops and pat dry. Trim off part of the fat, and cut meat slightly at bone to help to keep the chops from turning up during cooking. Sprinkle salt and pepper lightly on both sides of chops and dredge in 2 cups flour.

Heat oil in skillet over high heat; brown chops on both sides. Fry until golden brown. Remove chops from pan and place on a platter.

Sprinkle ⅓ cup flour into drippings; stir in, and let flour brown slightly. Stir in 1½ cups water, and continue stirring to make sure flour and water mix smoothly.

Note: This gravy is very good over mashed potatoes or rice and the pork chops.

Note: If you want extra-tender chops, place them back in the gravy, cover, and cook over low heat for a few more minutes.

Note: Pork chops are also very good cooked over medium heat without flouring them. Instead of oil, use margarine, keeping heat low enough so margarine doesn't burn. Cook several minutes on both sides until done; test with a small cut to make sure juices run clear.

Note: Pork chops are also good baked in the oven at 350° for about 45 minutes. Pour the drippings off the chops, and pour on a good barbecue sauce.

Yield: 2-3 servings

Pot Roast

1 teaspoon pepper
1 teaspoon salt
1 teaspoon seasoned salt
1 teaspoon garlic powder
1 (2 to 3-pound) boneless chuck or shoulder roast
oil
2 cups water
1 onion, quartered
3 large potatoes
4 carrots
1 cup water
$\frac{1}{4}$ cup self-rising flour
salt and pepper to taste

Sprinkle seasonings on both sides of roast, rubbing into meat. Place roast in Dutch oven or large covered skillet with just enough oil to keep from sticking. Brown roast on both sides over medium-high heat. Reduce heat, pour water over roast, and top with onion. Cover and simmer until tender ($1\frac{1}{2}$ to 2 hours).

While meat is cooking, peel potatoes and carrots, cut into pieces and set aside in a bowl or pan of cold water. When roast is tender, place potatoes and carrots on top of roast, and cook until tender (about 30 minutes). Place roast on a large platter, and surround with vegetables, alternating potatoes and carrots.

Combine 1 cup water and flour; stir until blended, and pour into hot liquid in pan. Cook over medium heat, stirring constantly until mixture is smooth and thickened; add salt and pepper to taste. Serve gravy with roast and vegetables.

Note: This gravy is also delicious served over an open biscuit. You might want to sprinkle more black pepper and salt into the gravy.

Note: You might like to add several peeled small onions with the potatoes and carrots. This really adds flavor to the dish.

Yield: 6-8 servings

Country-Fried Steak

½ teaspoon salt
½ teaspoon pepper
1½ cups self-rising flour
1 cup oil
4 to 6 pieces select cubed steak
1 medium onion, chopped
3 cups water

Combine salt, pepper, and flour in a shallow pan or on a platter. Flour steak on both sides; set remaining flour aside.

Heat oil in large skillet over medium-high heat; add steak and brown on both sides. Remove steak from skillet; reduce heat, and add onion. Saute onion until tender. Combine remaining flour and water; blend well. Pour flour mixture into skillet and stir slowly until gravy begins to thicken. Return steaks to skillet; cover and simmer over low heat 15 to 20 minutes.

Yield: 4-6 servings

Salisbury Steak

2 pounds extra-lean ground beef chuck
1½ cups finely chopped onion
2 eggs
2 tablespoons Worcestershire sauce
1 teaspoon seasoned salt
1 teaspoon pepper
1 teaspoon garlic salt
1 cup sifted self-rising flour
½ cup oil
1½ to 2 cups water

Combine first seven ingredients, and mix well. Shape mixture into 8 balls, pressing to ½-inch thickness; flour on both sides. Heat oil in a skillet; reduce heat to medium-high. Add meat patties and brown on both sides, cooking about 10 minutes. Remove patties from pan and set aside.

Mix remaining flour with water, and blend well. Add flour mixture to skillet, and stir until gravy thickens. Return patties to pan, reduce heat, and simmer 10 to 15 minutes.

Yield: 6-8 servings

Holiday Turkey Loaf

1 cup chicken broth
1 cup soft breadcrumbs
3 cups ground or finely chopped cooked turkey
3 tablespoons finely chopped onion
1/4 teaspoon pepper
2 eggs, slightly beaten
2 tablespoons chicken fat or margarine
1/2 cup finely chopped celery
2 teaspoons crushed sage
1 teaspoon salt

Combine all ingredients and mix thoroughly. Place mixture in greased loaf pan; bake at 350° for 1 hour or until firm.

Yield: 6 servings

For every minute you are angry, you lose sixty seconds of happiness.

— ANONYMOUS —

Baked Turkey
with Traditional Southern Cornbread Dressing

1 (10 to 12-pound) turkey
salt
margarine

Thaw turkey; remove giblets and neck, wash turkey, and drain. Sprinkle salt inside cavity and on outside skin and brush with salted margarine. Place turkey in roasting pan and wrap securely with heavy-duty aluminum foil, blousing foil so it doesn't stick to turkey while baking. Bake at 350° for 3 to 4 hours, depending on size of turkey. When done, remove from oven and loosen foil at one end of roasting pan so you can pour drippings into a pan. Mix drippings with enough water to make 2 cups; save broth for dressing.

Dressing

6 cups cornbread crumbs
2 cups biscuit crumbs
½ teaspoon salt
½ teaspoon pepper
1½ tablespoons rubbed sage
½ cup butter or margarine
1 medium onion, finely chopped
2 cups chopped celery
½ cup water
2 cups broth
½ cup vegetable oil
3 eggs, slightly beaten

Combine cornbread crumbs and biscuit crumbs in large bowl. Sprinkle seasonings over crumbs; set aside.

Combine margarine, onion, celery, and water in saucepan. Cook over medium heat until margarine is melted. Add onion mixture, broth, and oil to crumbs; stir well, mashing crumbs. Add eggs and stir until blended.

Pour mixture into baking dish or pan; bake at 350° about 35 to 40 minutes or until golden brown.

Note: This makes a very tasty moist dressing to serve with turkey.

Yield: 15 servings

Giblet Gravy

giblets (liver and gizzard) and neck from turkey
3 cups broth
2 to 3 hard-boiled eggs, chopped
4 tablespoons self-rising flour
1 cup water
salt and pepper to taste

Boil giblets and neck in water until very tender; drain and reserve broth. Chop giblets into small pieces, and pull meat from neck bone. Bring broth to a boil, and thicken with a mixture of flour and water; cook until thick. Add chopped giblets, neck meat, eggs, salt, and pepper to taste.

Note: Instead of using giblets to make the gravy, you can use the turkey wings or thighs.

Note: Cranberry sauce adds a delicious flavor to complete your dinner.

Yield: 5 cups

The most precious of all possessions is a wise and loyal friend.

— DARIUS —

Veal Parmigiana

2 eggs, beaten
1/4 teaspoon salt
1/4 teaspoon pepper
1/4 teaspoon garlic powder
6 or 8 veal cutlets (1/8-inch thick)
1 cup finely crushed dry breadcrumbs
1/3 cup light oil
2 (8-ounce) cans tomato sauce
1/4 cup Parmesan cheese
1/2 tablespoon oregano leaves
1 teaspoon pepper
2 tablespoons brown sugar
1 package (8-ounce) sliced or grated mozzarella cheese

Combine eggs, salt, pepper, and garlic powder in a bowl. Place cutlets into mixture, and let stand a few minutes, turning to coat each cutlet. Coat each cutlet with breadcrumbs. Heat oil in a skillet; add cutlets, and brown on both sides. Remove cutlets, and set aside.

Combine tomato sauce, Parmesan cheese, oregano leaves, pepper, and brown sugar in skillet. Heat to boiling, stirring frequently.

Place veal cutlets in baking dish; pour tomato sauce mixture over cutlets. Bake at 375° for 15 minutes; remove from oven, and top with mozzarella cheese. Bake an additional 15 to 20 minutes.

Yield: 6 to 8 servings

When friends meet, hearts warm.

— JOHN RAY —

Vegetable Beef Soup

- 1½ pounds lean stew beef, cut into small pieces
- 2 medium to large onions, halved and cut into very thin slices
- 4 stalks of celery, washed, stripped, and cut into thin slices
- ½ tablespoon salt
- 1 teaspoon pepper
- 1 teaspoon garlic powder
- 2½ quarts water
- 1 (16-ounce) bag small mixed frozen vegetables or ⅓ cup each lima beans, diced carrots, cut green beans, whole-kernel corn, green peas, and diced potatoes
- 1 large can diced tomatoes
- 1 large can tomato sauce

Place beef, onions, celery, salt, pepper, and garlic powder in large saucepan. Add 2½ quarts water, and bring to a boil; reduce heat to medium-low, and cook 1 hour. Cook vegetables separately until tender; drain. Add vegetables, tomatoes, and tomato sauce to meat mixture, and stir well. Simmer for 30 minutes.

Note: Add 1 cup of cooked elbow macaroni to give "body" to the soup.

Yield: 6-8 servings

Barbecue Wieners

1 to 2 pounds wieners

1 to 1½ cups good-flavored barbecue sauce

Cut each wiener into four equal pieces; cut an X in both ends of each piece. Put wieners in baking dish, and pour barbecue sauce over them. Cover and bake at 350° for 20 to 25 minutes.

Note: For a different hors d'oeuvre, serve wieners and barbecue sauce in a chafing dish. You might have to add extra barbecue sauce—if they last that long!

Yield: 6-8 servings

Baked Beans and Butterfly Wieners

1 pound all-meat or beef wieners

1 (1-pound) can pork and beans

Cut each wiener into four equal pieces; cut an X in both ends of each piece. Pour half of the pork and beans into baking dish; place the wieners on top, spacing them an inch or so apart. Pour the remaining pork and beans over the wieners; bake at 350° for 35 to 40 minutes.

Note: You can use more wieners if you want. You can also use the Baked Bean recipe on page 64 instead of the 1-pound can of pork and beans.

Yield: 6 to 8 servings

Salmon Croquettes

1 (16-ounce) can salmon
1 medium onion, finely chopped
1½ cups crushed saltines
2 eggs, beaten
¼ cup self-rising flour
oil

Place salmon in mixing bowl; remove skin and bones. Mash salmon to separate slightly. Add onion, saltines, eggs, and flour; stir until well blended.

Form mixture into balls in palm of hand (use about 2½ ounces of mixture for each ball). Heat oil in deep fryer or skillet; drop balls into hot oil and fry until brown. Drain in colander or on paper towels.

Note: The mixture can be pressed into patties as well.

Yield: 4 servings

Friendship consists in forgetting what one gives, and remembering what one receives.

— ALEXANDRE DUMAS —

Lime-Garlic Broiled Shrimp

2 pounds raw, peeled, deveined shrimp
3 cloves garlic, minced
½ cup butter or margarine, melted
2 tablespoons lime juice
½ teaspoon salt
dash of freshly ground pepper
chopped parsley

Thaw shrimp if frozen.

Cook garlic in butter until tender; remove from heat. Add lime juice, salt, and pepper.

Arrange shrimp in a single layer in a 15 x 10 x 1-inch baking pan. Pour sauce over shrimp.

Broil about 4 inches from heat for 8 to 10 minutes or until shrimp are pink and tender. Sprinkle with parsley.

Yield: 6-8 servings

Fried Shrimp

1½-2 pounds peeled and deveined shrimp
1 cup self-rising flour
¼ cup self-rising meal
½ teaspoon garlic salt
¼ teaspoon pepper
1½ cups vegetable oil
1 egg, beaten
1 cup water

Combine dry ingredients in a medium size bowl. Blend egg and water with whisk or fork in a separate bowl. Dip shrimp in egg mixture and roll in dry mixture. Heat oil in skillet and cook shrimp on each side for approximately 2 minutes. Drain in colander and repeat process until all shrimp are cooked. Serve with Billy's Cocktail Sauce on page 131.

Yield: 6-8 servings

Refreshing Scallop Salad

5 cups shredded lettuce
1 pound asparagus, cooked
1 pint cherry tomatoes, cut in half
3 hard-boiled eggs, sliced
1 cucumber, sliced
1 pound poached scallops
Louis Dressing

Place shredded lettuce in bottom of a large salad bowl. Line one-fourth edge of bowl with asparagus, one-fourth with tomatoes, and finish lining bowl with alternating slices of egg and cucumber. Fill the center of the bowl with scallops. Serve with Louis Dressing on page 130.

Yield: 5-6 servings

Baked Flounder

8 ounces fish fillets
1 tablespoon ketchup
1 teaspoon lemon juice
1 tablespoon melted fat or oil
1 tablespoon Worcestershire sauce
dash of pepper
chopped parsley

Place fish in a single layer in a well-greased 8 x 8 x 2-inch baking pan. Combine remaining ingredients except parsley; pour over fish. Bake at 350° for 20 to 25 minutes or until fish flakes easily when tested with a fork. Sprinkle with parsley.

Yield: 2 servings

Snapper Greek Style

4 (about 1½ pounds) snapper fillets
½ cup lemon juice
1 teaspoon thyme
½ teaspoon salt
½ cup melted butter
½ cup olive oil
1 teaspoon oregano
1 teaspoon pepper
¼ to ½ cup chopped green onions

Place fish in baking dish. Combine remaining ingredients, and pour over fish. Bake at 350° for 15 to 20 minutes or until fish flakes easily when tested with a fork.

Yield: 6 servings

Baked Red Snapper with Mushrooms

2 pounds skinless red snapper steaks
1 (4-ounce) can mushroom stems and pieces, drained
1 teaspoon grated onion
½ cup melted margarine or oil
2 tablespoons lemon juice
1 teaspoon salt
⅛ teaspoon salt and pepper
paprika

Thaw fish if frozen. Cut into serving-size portions, and place in a single layer in a well-greased 13 x 9 x 2-inch baking dish. Combine remaining ingredients except paprika, and pour over fish. Bake at 350° for 25 to 30 minutes or until fish flakes easily when tested with a fork. Sprinkle with paprika.

Yield: 6 servings

One-Pan Meals

Two are better than one; for if they fall,
the one will lift his fellow.

— ECCLESIASTES 4:9,10 KJV —

Chicken and Rice

1 tablespoon olive or vegetable oil
2 chicken thighs with legs or
2 breasts with wings
½ pound sweet or hot Italian sausage links
1 medium onion, chopped
1 large clove garlic, minced
1 cup uncooked long-grain rice
1 bay leaf
1½ cups chicken broth
1 cup frozen green peas, thawed
2 tablespoons slivered canned pimento or cayenne pepper

Heat oil in large skillet over high heat; reduce heat, add chicken and sausage, and brown well on all sides. Place cooked chicken and sausage on paper towels; cut sausage into 1-inch slices.

Discard all but 1 tablespoon drippings from skillet. Add onion and garlic to drippings; cook 1 minute. Stir in rice. Add bay leaf and chicken broth; heat to boiling.

Return chicken and sausage to skillet. Cover and cook over low heat until rice and chicken are almost tender. Add peas and pimento; cook until tender. Discard bay leaf.

Yield: 2 servings

Skillet Salmon

2 tablespoons vegetable oil
1 tablespoon butter or margarine
2 carrots, peeled and julienned
1 stalk celery, julienned
1 small onion, sliced
¼ cup water
½ teaspoon salt
2 (4 to 5-ounce) salmon fillets

Heat oil and butter or margarine in large skillet over medium heat. Add carrots, celery, and onion; saute until tender-crisp. Stir in water and salt.

Place salmon, skin side down, over vegetables. Cover skillet, and reduce heat to low.

Steam-cook salmon just until it's firm and flakes easily when tested with a fork.

Yield: 2 servings

Beef and Vegetable Stir-fry

- 3/4 pound boneless beef sirloin steak
- 1/2 cup beef broth
- 2 tablespoons soy sauce
- 1 tablespoon cornstarch
- 2 teaspoons sugar
- 1/2 teaspoon ground ginger
- 3 tablespoons vegetable oil
- 1/2 pound green beans, cut in half diagonally
- 2 small onions, cut into wedges
- 1/4 pound mushrooms, sliced

Freeze steak just until it's firm enough to slice easily. Trim and discard any excess fat from steak; cut steak crosswise into thin slices. Combine broth, soy sauce, cornstarch, sugar, and ginger in a small bowl. Heat a medium-size skillet; add 2 tablespoons oil, beans, and onions. Cook, stirring with a slotted spoon until crisp-tender. Add mushrooms; stir-fry until tender. Remove vegetables from heat; place in a bowl.

Add remaining oil to skillet; heat over high heat, and add beef. Stir-fry beef just until well browned; remove from heat and place on a plate.

Add cornstarch mixture to skillet; heat to boiling. Return vegetables to skillet; heat until hot. Stir in beef, and serve immediately.

Yield: 2 servings

They are rich who have true friends.

— THOMAS FULLER —

Pan-fried Pork Cutlets

- 4 (1/2-inch-thick) slices boneless pork loin or 4 thin rib pork chops, boned
- salt and pepper
- flour
- 1 tablespoon vegetable oil
- 1 small onion, chopped
- 1/2 cup chicken broth
- 2 teaspoons firmly packed brown sugar
- 2 teaspoons Dijon-style mustard

With meat mallet, pound pork slices or chops to 1/4-inch thickness. Sprinkle each cutlet with salt and pepper; dust with flour, shaking off excess. Heat oil in large skillet over medium heat. Add cutlets, and brown well on both sides. Remove from heat; place on a plate.

Add onion to skillet, and cook 1 minute. Stir in chicken broth; heat to boiling, stirring to loosen browned bits in the bottom of the pan. Add brown sugar and mustard, stirring until blended. Return pork with its juices to the skillet.

Yield: 2 servings

A friend is a person with whom I may be sincere; before whom I may think out loud.

— RALPH WALDO EMERSON —

Eggplant Mozzarella

2 large eggs
1/4 cup water
1 cup packaged seasoned breadcrumbs
1/2 cup flour
2 small eggplant
vegetable oil
1 (16-ounce) package mozzarella cheese
1 (16-ounce) jar spaghetti sauce

Combine eggs and water in a pie plate, beating well. Place breadcrumbs and flour on separate sheets of waxed paper. Trim ends off eggplant, and cut each crosswise into 1/3-inch thick slices.

Dip eggplant slices in flour and then into egg mixture; coat with breadcrumbs.

Heat 2 tablespoons oil in large skillet. Fry eggplant until tender and browned on both sides; if necessary, add more oil. Drain cooked eggplant on paper towels. After all eggplant slices have been fried, wipe skillet clean with paper towels. Cut mozzarella crosswise into 1/4-inch thick slices. Add spaghetti sauce to skillet; overlap eggplant and cheese slices over sauce. Cover skillet and cook over medium heat just until simmering and cheese melts. Let stand 10 minutes before serving.

Yield: 4 to 6 servings

Vegetable Griddle Omelet

3 tablespoons olive oil
1 small onion, finely chopped
1 small clove garlic, finely chopped
1 small red pepper, seeded and cut into strips
1 small green pepper, seeded and cut into strips
2 small zucchini, sliced
8 large eggs
1 cup Half & Half
1 teaspoon dried oregano
½ teaspoon salt
¼ teaspoon pepper
1 cup shredded Swiss cheese
¼ cup Parmesan cheese

Heat oil in a large skillet with an ovenproof handle over medium heat. Add onion and cook, stirring frequently, until tender but not browned. Add garlic, red and green peppers, and zucchini; cook, stirring occasionally, until vegetables are tender-crisp.

Combine eggs, Half & Half, oregano, salt, and pepper in a bowl; beat well. Sprinkle Swiss cheese over vegetables in skillet; pour egg mixture over vegetables. Increase heat to medium-high; cook frittata without stirring, until eggs begin to set, rotating skillet over heat source for even cooking.

Sprinkle with Parmesan cheese, and bake at 350° for 8 to 10 minutes. Cut into 4 wedges.

Yield: 4 servings

Home-Cooked Vegetables-Southern Style

The cafe's current owner, Mary Jo McMichael (left), with Fannie Flagg.

You know, sometimes people get the idea that if vegetables are not "fresh" they're not good. Or they might say, "I can open cans at home." Well, there's a lot more to it than that! The way foods are cooked has more to do with how they taste than whether they're fresh, frozen, or canned.

We use all the fresh vegetables we can buy. My husband insists on fresh potatoes, both white and sweet potatoes. You would be surprised how many eateries use instant mashed potatoes. There is a world of difference between instant and "real" potatoes. It takes a lot of time to peel, cook, drain, and mash white potatoes. To cook sweet potatoes, you wash them, cut off the woodlike ends, cook, drain, rinse with cold water, and let cool. When they're cool, they're easy to peel.

Some vegetables are not available all year long, but cabbage has always been available year-round. One day a lady came through the line asking about whether this or that was fresh. When she asked my servers if the cabbage was "fresh," they almost laughed out loud. I have never seen frozen or canned cabbage, except, of course, sauerkraut!

Fried Green Tomatoes

green tomatoes
1½ cups flour
½ cup cornmeal
½ teaspoon salt
½ teaspoon pepper
milk
1½ cups vegetable oil

Select the greenest tomatoes available. Wash, remove stem, and slice into ¼-inch slices; place in bowl or on platter.

Mix flour, cornmeal, salt, and pepper with just enough milk to make a thick batter (the consistency of pancake batter). Heat oil in skillet over high heat; reduce heat to medium-high. Dip tomato slices into batter, wiping against bowl to remove excess batter, and place in hot oil. When browned on both sides, remove from oil and place in colander to drain (this will keep tomatoes from becoming soggy). To serve, stand up tomatoes like wheels in a serving bowl.

Note: If you don't want to make the batter from scratch, use our ***Irondale Cafe Original Whistlestop™ Recipes Brand Fried Green Tomato Batter Mix****.*

Note: Another way to batter the green tomatoes is to dip them into beaten egg or buttermilk, drain off excess liquid, and dip them into a mixture of flour and cornmeal. Fry in bacon drippings or hot oil; drain in colander before serving.

Note: The tomatoes can also be deep-fried in hot oil until brown and then drained in colander.

Asparagus Casserole

1 (16-ounce) can asparagus spears, drained
1 (16-ounce) can green peas, drained
1 (7-ounce) can sliced water chestnuts, drained
1 to 2 (10-ounce) cans cream of mushroom soup
1 cup breadcrumbs
4 slices processed cheese

Layer half of asparagus, peas, water chestnuts, and soup in baking dish; repeat layers. Top with breadcrumbs. Bake at 350° for 20 to 25 minutes or until bubbly. Top with cheese; bake until cheese melts.

Note: Mushrooms may be added.

Yield: 8 servings

Baked Beans

3 strips bacon, cut into 1-inch pieces
1 medium onion, chopped
1 (32-ounce) large can pork and beans
1 cup brown sugar (light or dark)
1½ cups ketchup

Saute bacon and onion in skillet; drain. Combine bacon and onion with remaining ingredients in a bowl; mix well (make sure there are no lumps of sugar). Pour mixture into medium size baking pan or dish; bake at 350° for 30 minutes.

Yield: 6 to 8 servings

Low-Fat Baked Beans

1 (16-ounce) can pork and beans
2 tablespoons dark brown sugar
1 small onion, chopped
2 tablespoons ketchup
¼ teaspoon mustard

Combine all ingredients in bowl; mix well. Pour into baking dish; bake at 350° for 25 minutes.

Yield: 3 servings

Corn and Green Bean Delight

1 (16-ounce) can French-style green beans, drained
1 (12-ounce) can shoepeg corn, drained
½ cup chopped celery
½ cup chopped green pepper
½ cup chopped onion
½ cup sour cream
1 (10 ¾-ounce) cream of celery soup, undiluted
salt and pepper
½ (12-ounce) package round buttery crackers, crushed
½ cup butter or margarine, melted
¼ cup slivered or sliced almonds

Combine first 9 ingredients; mix well, and pour into a greased shallow 2-quart casserole dish. Combine cracker crumbs, butter, and almonds; spoon over green bean mixture. Bake at 350° for 45 minutes.

Yield: 6 servings

Friends should be preferred to kings.

— VOLTAIRE —

Cooked-Fresh Green Beans

2 pounds green beans
2 ounces salt pork
1 teaspoon salt
1 onion
1 potato

Break tips off green beans and break into 1½-inch lengths. Rinse with cold water and drain.

Combine water and salt pork in a large saucepan and bring to a boil. Add salt and bring to second boil. Add green beans, whole onion, and whole potato; reduce heat, and cook over medium heat for 1 hour or until beans are tender.

Note: If fresh green beans are not available, use 2 to 3 cans green beans, draining off liquid and adding them to the fresh boiling water. Cook as above, adding the onion and potato to enhance the flavor of the beans and take away the canned taste.

Note: When cooking fresh green beans, place new potatoes (small red potatoes) on top of beans, and cook until tender to give a unique taste. New potatoes are available in the spring. They do not cook to pieces like baking potatoes do.

Yield: 8 servings

Green Bean Casserole

6 cups Cooked-Fresh Green Beans
1 (10 ¾-ounce) can cream of mushroom soup
1 cup crushed saltines
½ cup grated cheese

Drain Cooked-Fresh Green Beans, and take out the salt pork, onion, and potato. Layer half of green beans, cream of mushroom soup, crushed saltines, and grated cheese; repeat layers. Bake at 350° until bubbly and cheese melts. Serve hot.

Note: For a different taste, add slivered almonds to the soup mixture.

Yield: 8-10 servings

Green Bean Casserole with French-fried Onions

- 1 (10 ¾-ounce) can cream of mushroom soup
- ½ cup milk
- 1 teaspoon soy sauce
- ¼ teaspoon pepper
- 4 cups Cooked-Fresh Green Beans
- 1 (2.8-ounce) can French-fried onions

Mix soup and milk in bowl until well blended; pour into a 1½-quart casserole dish. Add soy sauce and pepper. Stir in beans and half of onions; mix well. Bake at 350° for 25 minutes or until hot and bubbly; stir mixture and top with remaining onions. Bake for an additional 5 minutes or until onions are golden brown.

Note: Canned green beans may be used for this recipe, but drain them first.

Yield: 6 servings

Southern Corn Pudding

- 2 cups fresh corn cut from cob <u>or</u> 2 cups frozen whole-kernel corn
- 2 teaspoons sugar
- 1½ teaspoons salt
- ¼ teaspoon pepper
- 3 eggs, lightly beaten
- 2 tablespoons butter or margarine
- 2 cups milk
- fresh parsley

Combine corn, sugar, salt, and pepper; add eggs, and mix well. Heat butter and milk in a saucepan until butter melts. Add to corn mixture, and pour into a buttered 1-quart casserole dish. Place dish in a pan of hot water. Bake at 350° for 1 hour or until knife inserted in center comes out clean. Garnish with fresh parsley.

Yield: 6 servings

Cheese Grits

- 3 cups cooked grits
- 2 eggs, beaten
- 1/3 cup milk
- 1 teaspoon salt
- 1 teaspoon garlic powder
- 1 cup grated cheese
- 1/2 stick margarine or butter

Combine grits, eggs, milk, salt, and garlic powder; mix well. Cut margarine into bits, and stir into grits mixture. Add 2/3 cup of cheese, and pour into greased baking dish; sprinkle remaining cheese on top. Bake at 350° for 30 minutes.

Yield: 6 servings

Macaroni and Cheese

- 1 (8-ounce) package macaroni
- 3 tablespoons butter or margarine
- 2 cups milk
- 1 teaspoon salt
- 1 teaspoon pepper
- 1/2 pound grated cheddar cheese
- 3 eggs, slightly beaten

Cook macaroni in boiling salted water until tender; drain and rinse with cold water, leaving in colander to drain. Combine margarine, milk, and seasonings in saucepan; cook over medium-high heat until margarine melts. Let cool.

Layer half of macaroni in baking dish, and sprinkle with two-thirds of the grated cheese; top with remaining macaroni. Add eggs to the cooled milk mixture; beat with a wire whisk or cooking spoon. Pour over layered macaroni and cheese. Sprinkle remaining cheese over top; bake at 350° for 30 minutes or until set.

Note: For added crispness, add two-thirds cup breadcrumbs to the remaining cheese, and sprinkle the mixture over casserole.

Yield: 4-6 servings

Creamed Onions

6 to 8 medium onions
3 tablespoons flour
1½ cups milk
3 tablespoons margarine
salt and pepper

Peel and slice onions; cook in small amount of water until tender, and drain. Combine flour and milk in a saucepan, and blend well. Cook over medium heat until mixture starts to thicken. Add margarine and stir until melted. Add onions, and stir well. Add salt and pepper to taste.

Note: For cheesy onions, add 1 cup grated cheddar cheese, and stir until melted.

Yield: 8-10 servings

Spinach Casserole

2 eggs beaten
1 cup cream of mushroom soup
2 (12-ounce) boxes chopped spinach, cooked
2 onions, chopped
1 cup mayonnaise
breadcrumbs
butter

Combine eggs and soup in a buttered casserole dish. Add spinach, onions, and mayonnaise; mix well. Sprinkle breadcrumbs over top; dot with butter. Bake at 300° for 40 minutes.

Yield: 6-8 servings

Zucchini in Cream

- 6 medium unpeeled zucchini, cut into ½-inch slices
- ⅔ cup sour cream
- 2 tablespoons margarine or butter
- ⅔ cup grated sharp cheddar cheese
- ½ tablespoon seasoned salt
- 1 teaspoon pepper
- ½ cup crushed saltines or breadcrumbs

Cook zucchini in water for 12 minutes; drain and set aside. Place sour cream, cheese, margarine, seasoned salt, and pepper in saucepan; cook over medium heat until cheese melts and spices and cheese are blended into sour cream, stirring often.

Layer half of zucchini, sour cream mixture, and breadcrumbs in a casserole dish; repeat layers. Bake at 350° for 10 to 15 minutes or until breadcrumbs are slightly brown.

Yield: 6-8 servings

Harvard Beets

- 3 tablespoons sugar
- 1 tablespoon cornstarch
- ½ cup water
- ¼ cup vinegar
- 1 tablespoon butter or margarine
- 1½ pounds fresh beets, cooked
- ½ teaspoon salt

Combine sugar and cornstarch in a medium saucepan, stirring well. Gradually add water and stir until smooth. Add vinegar and butter, and cook over medium heat, stirring constantly until butter melts and mixture thickens. Add beets and salt; cook 5 minutes or until beets are thoroughly heated.

Note: You can use 1 large can sliced beets if fresh beets are not available. Use the liquid from the beets instead of water, and make the thickened sauce as directed above.

Yield: 4 servings

Mashed Potatoes

4 medium potatoes, peeled and quartered
½ cup milk
¼ cup butter
1½ teaspoons salt
¼ teaspoon pepper

Cook potatoes in boiling water 15-20 minutes; drain. Remove from pan and mash well. Add remaining ingredients and blend well.

Yield: 4 servings

Scalloped Potatoes

5 medium baking potatoes, thinly sliced and parboiled
1 (10-ounce) can cream of mushroom soup
1 cup (or more) shredded sharp cheddar cheese
1 small onion, finely chopped
2 tablespoons margarine

Layer half of potatoes, soup, and cheese in baking dish; sprinkle with onion, and repeat layers; dot with margarine. Bake at 300° for 1 hour.

Yield: 8 servings

Stewed Fresh Potatoes

8 to 10 small new potatoes or 4 large cobbler potatoes
1 teaspoon salt
½ stick margarine
1 teaspoon pepper
4 tablespoons flour
1 cup water

Peel potatoes; wash and cut into chunks (cut small potatoes in half; cut larger ones into 6 to 8 pieces). Place in saucepan, and cover with water. Add salt, and cook 25 to 30 minutes.

When potatoes are tender, add margarine and pepper. Combine flour and water; blend well, and add to potato mixture, stirring well so mixture does not lump.

Yield: 8-10 servings

Candied Yams

3 to 3½ pounds sweet potatoes
1 cup sugar
1½ tablespoons cornstarch
2 cups water
½ cup margarine
2 teaspoons vanilla extract

Wash potatoes thoroughly; cut off woody end, do not peel. Place potatoes in saucepan, cover with water and cook 30 to 40 minutes (do not overcook); drain. Rinse potatoes with cold water until they are cool enough to handle. Peel potatoes, and set aside.

Combine sugar and cornstarch in saucepan (this makes it easier to blend the cornstarch and water). Add 2 cups water, and stir until blended. Place over high heat; reduce heat to medium when water gets hot. Add margarine, stirring often until mixture starts to thicken. When mixture is thick, remove from heat, and add vanilla.

Note: You can cut the cooked potatoes into chunks or slices and place them in baking dish, layering if needed. Pour thickened mixture over potatoes and bake at 350° for 25 minutes.

Yield: 10-12 servings

Sweet Potato Puffs

1½ pounds sweet potatoes, cooked and mashed
2 tablespoons margarine, melted
⅓ cup firmly packed brown sugar
½ teaspoon cinnamon
1 teaspoon vanilla extract
8 large marshmallows
2 cups cornflakes, crushed

Combine sweet potatoes, margarine, brown sugar, cinnamon, and vanilla; chill. Form balls around marshmallows with potato mixture and roll in cornflakes. Fry in skillet until brown.

Yield: 8 puffs

Crunchy Sweet Potato Casserole

3 cups mashed cooked sweet potatoes
1 cup sugar
2 eggs
½ cup evaporated milk
½ cup melted butter
1 teaspoon vanilla extract
1 cup packed brown sugar
⅓ cup flour
⅓ cup melted butter
½ to 1 cup chopped pecans

Combine sweet potatoes, sugar, eggs, evaporated milk, butter, and vanilla in bowl; mix well, and spoon into baking dish. Combine brown sugar, flour, ⅓ cup butter, and pecans in bowl; spread over sweet potato mixture. Bake at 350° for 30 minutes.

Note: You can substitute milk for the evaporated milk.

Yield: 8-10 servings

Sweet Potato Soufflé

3 pounds sweet potatoes
½ cup margarine, softened
½ cup brown sugar
¼ cup granulated sugar
2 teaspoons vanilla
½ teaspoon ground cinnamon
½ teaspoon ground nutmeg
large marshmallows

Wash and scrub sweet potatoes, and place them in a saucepan. Cover potatoes with water, and bring to a boil; reduce heat to medium-high and cook about 40 minutes. Stick the potatoes with a sharp knife to test for doneness; the potatoes need to be cooked a little longer for soufflé than for candied yams.

When potatoes are done, drain and rinse with cold water until cool enough to handle. Peel and place in mixing bowl. Add margarine and mash with a potato masher. Add brown sugar, granulated sugar, vanilla, cinnamon, and nutmeg; mix with an electric mixer until smooth. Pour into baking dish and bake at 350° for 15 to 20 minutes or until hot. Remove from oven and cover with marshmallows; return to oven long enough for marshmallows to start melting and brown slightly.

Note: If the potatoes are cold when you put them into the oven, you might want to cover them with foil while heating to prevent overcooking.

Yield: 10-12 servings

Broccoli Casserole

3-4 cups cooked broccoli
1 (10-ounce) can cream of mushroom soup
1 cup saltines, crushed
1½ cups grated cheese

Cut cooked broccoli into pieces, and arrange in baking dish; top with half of soup, crushed saltines, and grated cheese. Repeat layers, ending with cheese. Bake at 350° until bubbly and cheese melts.

Note: To cook fresh broccoli, trim off large leaves and tough stems. Place broccoli in a saucepan; add a small amount of water and 1 teaspoon salt. Cook for 15 minutes or until tender. Drizzle with melted margarine and serve hot.

Yield: 4-6 servings

Cooked-Fresh Okra

Use very fresh pods of okra; wash and remove stems. If boiling, be careful not to cut into pod or okra will become slimy. Place 1 pound okra and 1 teaspoon salt into saucepan; cover with water, and cook over medium heat for about 10 minutes. Drain and serve with melted margarine and 1 tablespoon lemon juice.

For the best fried okra, wash okra and remove stems; cut into ½-inch pieces, and place in a bowl. Sprinkle a small amount of water over okra so it will be damp but not wet. Sift flour over okra, tossing to coat well; keep tossing okra while you are waiting to cook it. Place vegetable oil into frying pan and heat over high heat; reduce heat to medium-high. Sift okra through fingers onto a plate; rake okra into frying pan (be sure not to crowd okra in the frying pan so it will get brown and not mushy). Let okra start to brown before stirring so the flour will not come off okra. With slotted spoon or spatula, remove okra when brown, and drain in a colander. Repeat until all okra is fried. Sprinkle salt over okra while hot.

Note: Rather than draining on paper towels as some recipes call for, use a colander. It lets the okra drain without letting it get soggy. The oil can be strained and used to fry more okra later.

Yield: 1 pound makes 4 servings

Southern Fried Corn

6 ears corn
1 cup water or milk
2 to 3 slices bacon or salt pork
1 teaspoon sugar
salt and pepper

Remove husks from corn, breaking off stems; remove silks with a stiff vegetable brush, and wash with cold water. Using a sharp knife, cut a thin layer off the kernels; cut again, and scrape the rest of the juices into bowl, firmly placing knife on cob and scraping into bowl. Add water or milk, and stir well.

Fry bacon or salt pork in a large skillet; remove meat, and add corn to skillet. Cook over medium heat for 10 to 15 minutes, stirring often (cook fresh picked corn a few extra minutes or until corn is thick). Add sugar and salt and pepper to taste.

Note: If fresh corn is not available, use frozen whole-kernel corn (shoepeg, if available). Cook corn according to package directions a few minutes; place corn and water into a blender and puree. (Be careful not to put too much into blender; the corn can splash out and burn you.) Repeat procedure 3 times, each time pouring corn back into pot and scooping out more. Combine flour and water until blended; pour into pureed corn and cook several minutes, stirring constantly until mixture thickens. Add salt and pepper to taste. This tastes like fresh corn that has been scraped from the cob.

Note: For a different taste, add chopped ripe tomatoes to the corn before serving it.

Yield: 4-6 servings

I can live for two months on one good compliment.

— MARK TWAIN —

Cooked Fresh Corn on the Cob

Clean off silks and rinse corn well. Drop the corn (whole or cut in half) into boiling salted water and boil 10 minutes, or until tender. Rub or brush margarine on corn and sprinkle with salt to taste.

Cooked Dried Beans

- 2 cups Great Northern, pinto, lima, or navy beans
- 1 (1½-ounce) piece salt pork or streak-of-lean
- 4½ to 5 cups water
- 1 teaspoon salt

Pour out a few beans at a time onto a small plate and look them over; discard any with holes in them. Place beans in a large bowl, and cover with hot water 2 or 3 inches above beans, Keep beans covered well.

Cut an X across the center of each piece of salt pork, but not through rind. Rinse salt pork and place in a large pot or Dutch oven, with 4½ to 5 cups water and salt. Bring to a boil.

By this time, the dried beans you are soaking in hot water have swelled considerably. Pour beans into a colander and drain; rinse with hot water.

Place beans into boiling water; return to a boil, reduce heat to medium-low and cook 2 hours or until beans are tender.

Yield: 6 servings

Note: Streak-of-lean is presliced, packaged salt pork.

Note: When cooking Great Northern beans, add a teaspoon of garlic powder for more flavor.

Note: A ham hock, instead of salt pork, is very good, especially with large lima beans or black-eyed peas.

Cooked Cabbage

1 head cabbage
1 (1-ounce) piece salt pork
1 tablespoon vegetable oil
1 teaspoon salt
water

Peel off outer leaves of cabbage; cut out core with a sharp knife and discard. Cut cabbage into quarters, and cut each quarter in half. Wash cabbage in cold water; drain well.

Slice salt pork very thin; place in large saucepan with oil and fry over medium-high heat, being careful not to burn meat. Add water and salt and bring to a boil. Add cabbage; cover, reduce heat and simmer until tender. Do not overcook.

Note: If you do not want to season with salt pork, cook cabbage as directed above, drain and stir in 1 tablespoon margarine.

Note: Another way to enhance the flavor of cabbage is to cook a thinly sliced onion with the cabbage.

Yield: 4-6 servings

Cabbage and Noodle Dish

1 (16-ounce) package wide noodles
1 large onion, chopped
1 cup margarine
1 large head cabbage, shredded
1 teaspoon salt
pepper

Cook noodles according to package directions; drain. Saute onion in margarine in saucepan; add cabbage and cook until cabbage is tender. Add noodles; toss to mix well. Season with salt and pepper and cook until thoroughly heated.

Yield: 4-6 servings

Southern Turnip Greens

1 large bunch turnip greens
2 ounces streak-of-lean or salt pork belly
2 quarts water
1 teaspoon salt
1 teaspoon sugar
cornbread

Clean greens by breaking off any large stems below the leaf, discarding any yellow or wilted leaves. Wash well by plunging greens up and down in sink or large pan of water. Take greens completely out of water each time and rinse sink or pan to remove sand before refilling. Repeat procedure several times; put leaves in colander to drain, making sure there is no sand in final water. Cut greens in half.

Rinse salt pork, cube, and place in a large pot with 2 quarts water, salt, and sugar; bring to boil. Add turnip greens; bring back to a boil. Reduce heat to medium and cook 2 hours or until greens are tender. Serve the greens in bowls with some pot liquor and crumbled cornbread. Or drain the greens before serving with crumbled cornbread.

Note: Streak-of-lean is presliced, packaged salt pork.

Note: If the greens have the roots with them, peel, cut, and wash the roots; set aside. Add the roots to the pot during the last 45 minutes of cooking, making sure they are covered with water. They make a delicious addition to the greens.

Yield: 4-6 servings

Cooked Fresh Lima Beans or Butter Beans

4 cups shelled beans
5 cups water
1 ounce salt pork or drippings from 2 slices bacon
1 teaspoon salt

Wash shelled beans in cold water; drain. Place 5 cups water in large saucepan; add salt and salt pork or bacon drippings. Bring to a boil; add beans. Reduce heat to medium and cook for about 1 hour or until beans are tender. Check beans during cooking, and add enough water to cover them so they don't get mushy.

Note: You can use the same procedure for crowder peas, black-eyed peas, field peas, and lady peas.

Yield: 6-8 servings

Cooked Yellow Squash

2 pounds yellow squash, sliced
1 cup chopped onion
1 cup water
½ teaspoon salt
½ stick margarine
pepper

Combine squash, onion, water, and salt in a saucepan. Bring to a boil, reduce heat, and simmer 25 to 30 minutes or until squash is tender. Drain and mash. Season with ½ stick margarine and pepper to taste.

Yield: 4-6 servings

Squash Casserole

3 cups Cooked Yellow Squash
1 cup shredded cheddar cheese
1 cup crushed saltines
2 eggs, slightly beaten

Combine all ingredients in a bowl, mix well. Pour into a baking dish and bake at 350° for 30 minutes or until brown.

Yield: 6-8 servings

Squash Croquettes

3 cups Cooked Yellow Squash, drained
2 egg yolks
1 cup finely crushed saltines
¼ cup flour
2 egg whites

Place Cooked Yellow Squash mixture in a bowl and mash. Add egg yolks, saltines, and flour; stir well.

Beat egg whites until stiff. Fold into squash mixture and drop by spoonfuls into hot oil. Fry until golden brown; drain in a colander.

Yield: 6-8 servings

Squash Dressing

2 cups mashed Cooked Yellow Squash
2 cups crumbled cornbread
2 eggs, beaten
1 large onion, chopped
1 (10-ounce) can cream of chicken soup
½ cup melted butter
pepper to taste

Combine all ingredients in a bowl; mix well. Spoon into buttered baking dish and bake at 325° for 45 minutes.

Yield: 10-12 servings

Easy Fettuccini Alfredo

1 (12-ounce) package fettuccini
½ cup butter
1 cup freshly grated Parmesan cheese
1 (5-ounce) can evaporated milk

Cook pasta according to package directions; drain. Add butter, Parmesan cheese, and evaporated milk; toss to mix well. Serve immediately.

Yield: 6-8 servings

A father is a treasure, a brother a comfort, but a friend is both.

— BENJAMIN FRANKLIN —

Spinach Lasagna

- 2 cups nonfat cottage cheese
- 3 cups shredded low-fat mozzarella cheese
- 1/2 to 1 cup grated Parmesan cheese
- 1 (10-ounce) package frozen chopped spinach
- 1 (27-ounce) jar spaghetti sauce
- 1/4 cup water
- 6 to 9 uncooked lasagna noodles

Mix cottage cheese, mozzarella cheese, and Parmesan cheese in bowl; set aside. Cook spinach according to package directions; drain. Heat spaghetti sauce and water in saucepan; add spinach and simmer for 15 minutes. Spread one-third of the spinach sauce in a 9 x 13-inch baking dish. Layer half of uncooked noodles, cheese mixture, and remaining spinach sauce in prepared dish; repeat layers. Bake, covered with foil, at 325° for 45 minutes. Uncover and bake an additional 15 minutes. Let stand for 10 minutes before serving.

Yield: 6-8 servings

Green Chili and Rice Casserole

- 1 cup uncooked rice
- 1 (10-ounce) can cream of celery soup
- 1 cup sour cream
- 1 (4-ounce) can chopped green chilies
- 1/2 cup shredded cheddar cheese

Cook rice according to package directions. Add soup, sour cream, and green chilies; mix well. Spoon into baking dish; top with cheese. Bake, covered, at 350° for 45 minutes.

Yield: 2-4 servings

The most I can do for my friend is simply to be his friend.

— HENRY DAVID THOREAU —

Salads

Onion and Cucumber Salad

2 medium onions
3 medium cucumbers
1 cup sour cream
½ tablespoon seasoned salt
1 teaspoon pepper

Peel and slice onions, and break into onion rings. Wash cucumbers, and cut into thin slices. Combine onion rings and cucumber slices with sour cream and spices in a large bowl. Refrigerate and serve cold. Ummmmm good!

Yield: 4-6 servings

Pinto Bean Salad

5 cups cooked pinto beans
1 cup chopped red onions
1½ cups diced celery
½ cup minced parsley
1½ cups Italian salad dressing
dash of salt
dash of white pepper
dash of Tabasco

Combine all ingredients in a bowl and chill several hours or overnight. Garnish with celery leaves and parsley sprigs.

Yield: 8-10 servings

A true friend thinks of you when all others are thinking of themselves.

— ANONYMOUS —

Broccoli Delight Salad

- 1 cup mayonnaise
- 2 tablespoons apple cider vinegar
- ½ tablespoon sugar
- 2 stalks broccoli florets
- ½ cup raisins
- ½ cup chopped purple or red onion
- ½ cup chopped pecans
- 12 slices bacon, fried and crumbled
- ⅓ cup sunflower seeds, optional

Combine mayonnaise, vinegar, and sugar in a small bowl; mix well and chill overnight. Combine broccoli, raisins, onion, and pecans in a large bowl. Add dressing and mix well. Garnish with bacon.

Yield: 10 servings

Marinated Vegetable Salad

- 1 (16-ounce) can cut green beans, drained
- 1 (16-ounce) can green peas, drained
- 1 (16-ounce) can whole kernel corn, drained
- 2 cups celery, chopped
- 1 (4-ounce) jar chopped pimentos, drained
- ½ tablespoon salt
- 1 cup vinegar
- ½ cup oil
- 1 teaspoon paprika
- 1 cup sugar

Combine all vegetables and salt in a large bowl; mix gently and chill 1 hour. Drain well and add vinegar, oil, and sugar; mix gently, cover, and chill for several hours.

Yield: 12 servings

Low-Fat Carrot Salad

6 large carrots, grated
3/4 cup raisins
1 (16-ounce) can diced pineapple

Combine all ingredients in a bowl; mix well. Chill until served.

Yield: 12 servings

Cornbread Salad

1 package cornbread mix
2 small onions, chopped
2 small green bell peppers, chopped
1 cup celery, chopped
5 tomatoes, chopped
8 ounces bacon, fried
3/4 cup pickle relish
1 1/2 cups mayonnaise
1 tablespoon sugar

Cook cornbread according to package directions, trim off edges and crumble into bowl. Add onions, bell peppers, celery, tomatoes and bacon; mix gently.

Combine remaining ingredients in a separate bowl and mix well. Add to salad mixture and toss gently. Chill overnight.

Yield: 10-12 servings

Potato Salad

6 medium cobbler potatoes
3 hard-boiled eggs
1 onion, finely chopped (optional)
1 cup finely chopped celery
1/2 cup finely chopped bell pepper
1 teaspoon salt
1 teaspoon black pepper
1/2 cup mayonnaise
1/2 tablespoon mustard

Cook potatoes with skins on; peel and cube. Chop eggs, and combine with remaining ingredients in a large bowl. Add potatoes, and mix well. Serve warm or refrigerate and serve cold.

Yield: 8-10 servings

Frozen Fruit Salad

1 envelope unflavored gelatin
1/4 cup hot water
1 (1-pound) can fruit cocktail
1/2 cup mayonnaise
1 cup whipping cream, whipped

Dissolve gelatin in hot water; let cool slightly. Add fruit cocktail with syrup, and stir. Fold in mayonnaise and whipped cream. Pour into small loaf pan or Pyrex dish, and freeze just until firm. Slice and serve on a lettuce leaf.

Yield: 4-6 servings

Pear Salad with Lime Jell-O

1 large package lime Jell-O
1 (2 1/2-pound) can pears
1 (6-ounce) package softened cream cheese
2 tablespoons milk or cream
1 small bottle maraschino cherries

Dissolve Jell-O according to directions on package, substituting 1/2 cup liquid from pears for 1/2 cup water. Refrigerate until partially set.

Combine cream cheese and milk or cream; mix until smooth. Stuff each pear half with softened cream cheese. Place thin layer of Jell-O in bottom of rectangular glass dish. Place stuffed pear halves in Jell-O; place a cherry in center of each. Pour remaining Jell-O over pears; refrigerate until firm. Serve on lettuce.

Note: This is especially beautiful at Christmas time.

Yield: 10-12 servings

Hot Pineapple Salad

1 (20-ounce) can pineapple chunks, drained and juice reserved
½ cup sugar
1 cup shredded cheddar cheese
3 tablespoons all-purpose flour
3 tablespoons reserved pineapple juice
¼ cup butter or margarine, melted
12 ounces buttery crackers, crushed

Combine all ingredients except cracker crumbs and margarine and place in a buttered 1½-quart casserole dish. Top with cracker crumbs and margarine. Bake at 350° for 25 minutes.

Yield: 10-12 servings

Fruit Salad

2 large Delicious apples, peeled and chopped
3 large bananas, peeled and sliced
½ cup chopped pecans
½ cup raisins
½ cup finely chopped celery (use a small amount of celery leaves, finely chopped)
¼ cup sugar
⅔ cup mayonnaise

Combine first 5 ingredients in large mixing bowl; add sugar and mayonnaise, stirring gently until blended. Chill before serving.

Yield: 6-8 servings

Ambrosia

12 large seedless oranges, peeled, sectioned, and halved
1 coconut, cracked, peeled, and grated or 1 pound Snowflake coconut
½ cup sugar

Combine all ingredients in a large serving bowl, and mix well. Cover and refrigerate overnight.

Serve chilled.

Yield: 10-12 servings

Special Ambrosia

- 4 large oranges, peeled, seeded, and sectioned
- 2 large or 3 medium bananas, peeled and sliced
- 1 large can pineapple tidbits, drained and juice reserved
- 1 pound frozen shredded coconut
- 2/3 cup sugar

Layer orange sections, bananas, pineapple, coconut, and sugar in large glass serving bowl. Repeat layers, reserving 2 tablespoons coconut; pour reserved pineapple juice over top, and sprinkle with reserved coconut. Cover and refrigerate overnight. Serve chilled.

Note: The pineapple juice keeps the bananas from turning dark.

Yield: 10-12 servings

Jell-O Ambrosia

- 1 large can fruit cocktail
- 1 large container Cool Whip
- 1 small box peach Jell-O (or other flavor)

Drain fruit cocktail. Sprinkle dry Jell-O over fruit cocktail, and mix. Combine mixture with Cool Whip, mixing well; chill.

Note: I sometimes use Lite Cool Whip, sugar-free Jell-O, and fruit in its own juice or light syrup.

Yield: 6-8 servings

Quick Tuna Salad

- 1 (7-ounce) can tuna, drained
- 1/3 cup chopped dill pickle
- 1/4 teaspoon celery seeds
- seasoned salt to taste
- 1/4 teaspoon mustard
- 2 tablespoons mayonnaise

Combine tuna, pickle, celery seeds, seasoned salt, and mustard in bowl. Add mayonnaise; mix with fork.

Yield: 4-6 servings

Marinated Cabbage Slaw

1 large or 2 small heads cabbage, finely chopped
2 large onions, thinly sliced and separated into rings
2 green bell peppers, thinly sliced
3/4 cups sugar
Hot Dressing

Combine cabbage, onions, and bell pepper; sprinkle with sugar. Pour Hot Dressing over slaw.

Hot Dressing

2 teaspoons sugar
2 cups white vinegar
1 teaspoon celery seed (or more, up to 1 tablespoon)
2 teaspoons dry mustard
3/4 cup salad oil
pepper to taste

Combine all ingredients in a saucepan. Bring to a rolling boil, stirring constantly. Pour over cabbage mixture, and cover. Immediately refrigerate; chill for at least 4 hours. Toss well before serving.

Yield: 10-12 servings

Connie's Pasta Salad

3 cups rotini or tri-colored pasta
1/4 cup diced onion
1/3 cup diced bell pepper
1/3 cup diced red bell pepper
1 cup whole-kernel corn
1/2 cup English peas
3/4 cup low-fat Italian dressing
1/4 cup fat-free Parmesan cheese
1 teaspoon garlic powder
1 teaspoon Mrs. Dash

Cook pasta according to package directions; drain. Combine all ingredients in a large bowl and toss, making sure to evenly coat pasta; chill.

Yield: 6-8 servings

Chapter 4

Smells Like Home-
Fresh Baked Breads

Biscuits

Muffins

Special Breads

Cornbreads

All is well with him who is beloved of his neighbors.

— GEORGE HERBERT —

Biscuits

Buttermilk Biscuits

2 cups self-rising flour
1½ teaspoons baking powder
2 teaspoons sugar
¼ cup vegetable oil
¾ to 1 cup buttermilk
melted butter or margarine (optional)

Combine flour, baking powder, and sugar in a mixing bowl; stir together, raking flour up sides of bowl to form a hole. Pour buttermilk and oil into hole, and gently stir flour into liquids. Mix until flour is completely blended with liquids. Dough should be moist but not sticky.

Turn out dough onto floured surface and knead several times. Roll out dough to ½-inch thickness, and cut with biscuit cutter. Knead remaining dough 2 or 3 times, and repeat procedure until all dough is used.

Bake biscuits on lightly greased baking sheet at 450° for 12 to 15 minutes or until lightly brown. Brush with melted butter or margarine, if desired.

Note: The dough can be refrigerated overnight in an airtight container.

Yield: 10 to 12 biscuits

Cream Biscuits

2 cups self-rising flour
1 cup plus ¼ tablespoon whipping cream (not whipped)
melted butter or margarine (optional)

Combine flour and whipping cream in a bowl, and mix well; dough should be moist. Turn out dough onto lightly floured surface, and knead several times. Roll out dough to ½-inch thickness and cut with a biscuit cutter without turning cutter.

Bake on ungreased baking sheet at 450° for 10 to 12 minutes or until brown. Brush with melted butter or margarine, if desired.

Note: Biscuits can be made using 2¼ cups self-rising flour and 1 cup Half & Half. Both recipes make light, fluffy biscuits.

Note: For crustier biscuits, place them 1 inch apart on baking sheet to allow the biscuits to brown slightly on all sides. If you like soft edges, place the biscuits closer together on baking sheet.

Yield: 10-12 biscuits

Cheese-Garlic Biscuits

2 cups self-rising flour
1½ teaspoons baking powder
2 teaspoons sugar
¼ cup vegetable oil (canola oil works best)
¾ to 1 cup milk
¼ cup shredded cheddar cheese
⅓ cup margarine, melted and mixed with ½ teaspoon garlic powder

Combine flour, baking powder, sugar, and shredded cheese in a large bowl; stir to mix well. Add milk and oil, stirring gently until well mixed; dough should be moist but not sticky.

Turn out dough onto floured surface and knead several times. Roll out dough to ½-inch thickness, and cut with biscuit cutter. Knead remaining dough 2 or 3 times, and repeat procedure until all dough is used.

Place biscuits 2 inches apart on lightly greased baking sheet. Bake at 450° for 12 to 15 minutes or until lightly browned. As soon as you take the biscuits out of the oven, brush them with the garlic-flavored butter. Serve hot.

Note: You may substitute 2 cups baking mix for the 2 cups self-rising flour and 1½ teaspoons baking powder.

Yield: 10-12 biscuits

Light Biscuits

1 cup self-rising flour
3 tablespoons vegetable oil
¼ cup skim milk

Combine all ingredients and mix well. Turn out dough onto lightly floured surface and knead several times. Roll out to ¼-inch thickness, and cut without turning biscuit cutter.

Bake at 425° for 10 to 12 minutes.

Yield: 5-6 biscuits

Muffins

A friend is a present you give yourself.

— ROBERT LOUIS STEVENSON —

Mini Sour Cream Muffins

1 cup margarine, softened
8 ounces light sour cream
2 cups self-rising flour

Combine margarine and sour cream, mixing until smooth. Stir in flour, and blend well. Spoon into small muffin tins, using 1 tablespoon batter for each muffin. Bake at 350° for about 30 minutes or until brown.

Yield: 10 muffins

Tex-Mex Corn Muffins

1½ cups yellow cornmeal
½ teaspoon baking soda
½ teaspoon salt
1 cup shredded cheddar cheese
½ cup finely chopped onion
¼ cup chopped green chiles
2 eggs, lightly beaten
¼ cup corn oil
1 (8-ounce) can cream-style yellow corn
1 cup buttermilk

Combine cornmeal, baking soda, and salt in bowl. Stir in cheese, onion, green chiles, and eggs. Add buttermilk, corn oil, and corn; mix just until moistened. Fill preheated greased muffin cups three-fourths full. Bake at 400° for 30 minutes or until golden brown. Remove from muffin cups immediately.

Yield: 18 muffins

Low-Fat One-Two-Three Muffins

2 cups self-rising flour
2 tablespoons sugar
3 tablespoons mayonnaise
1 cup milk

Combine flour, sugar, and mayonnaise in bowl. Add milk; mix well. Spoon into greased muffin cups. Bake at 350° for 20 minutes or until brown.

Note: To make Cornbread Muffins, substitute 1 cup self-rising cornmeal for 1 cup of the self-rising flour.

Yield: 12 servings

Friendship is like money: easier made than kept.

— SAMUEL BUTLER —

The supreme happiness of life is the conviction that we are loved.

— VICTOR HUGO —

Special Breads

Billy's Original Hush Puppy Recipe

1 cup self-rising flour
2 cups self-rising cornmeal
3 tablespoons sugar
1½ tablespoons baking powder
4 tablespoons oil
2 eggs, beaten
1 large onion, finely chopped
1 jalapeno pepper, finely chopped or ground in food processor
1 cup buttermilk

Combine flour, cornmeal, sugar, and baking powder in a large bowl, and mix well.

Combine oil, eggs, onion, pepper, and buttermilk, stirring well. Add to dry mixture, and mix well. Batter will be stiff.

Use 2 tablespoons of batter (or an ice-cream scoop) to form each hush puppy.

Drop into hot oil (350°), and fry approximately 4 minutes or until brown.

Yield: 20-25 hush puppies

Pumpkin Bread

1 teaspoon nutmeg
1½ teaspoons salt
1 cup chopped pecans
2 teaspoons cinnamon
3½ cups all-purpose flour
3 cups sugar
2 teaspoons soda
½ teaspoon ginger
4 eggs
1 cup vegetable oil
1 pound canned pumpkin

Combine first 8 ingredients. Beat together eggs, oil, and pumpkin; add to dry mixture, and mix well.

Bake in a greased and floured 13 x 9 x 2-inch pan at 350° for 45 minutes.

Yield: 24 servings

Quick Sour Cream Coffee Cake

1 (2-layer) package yellow cake mix
1 cup sour cream
3/4 cup vegetable oil
1/2 cup sugar
4 eggs
3 tablespoons brown sugar
2 teaspoons cinnamon
1 cup chopped pecans
confectioners' sugar
milk

Combine cake mix, sour cream, oil, sugar, and eggs in a bowl; mix well. Combine brown sugar, cinnamon, and pecans in a small bowl; mix well. Alternate layers of batter and pecan mixture, half at a time, in a greased and floured tube pan. Bake at 350° for 1 hour. Let cool in pan 5 to 10 minutes; invert onto serving plate. Blend desired amounts of confectioners' sugar and milk in a small bowl. Drizzle over coffee cake.

Yield: 10-12 servings

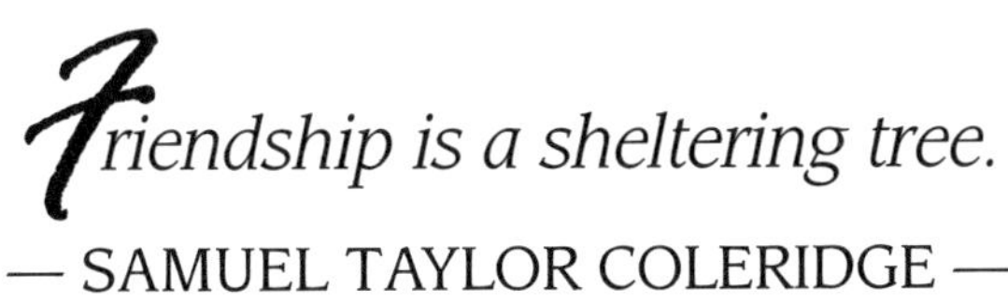

We make a living by what we get,
but we make a life by what we give.

— WINSTON CHURCHILL —

Cornbreads

Old-fashioned Cornbread

3 cups self-rising cornmeal
1 cup self-rising flour
2 teaspoons baking powder (optional)
3 eggs
4 cups buttermilk
2/3 cup bacon drippings or vegetable oil
2 teaspoons sugar (optional)

Sift together dry ingredients into mixing bowl. Beat eggs; add buttermilk, bacon drippings, and oil (do not use <u>hot</u> bacon drippings or <u>hot</u> oil). Add egg mixture to dry mixture, stirring well.

Pour mixture into muffin tins, a regular loaf pan, or a preheated cast-iron skillet. To preheat the skillet, pour a small amount of oil into the skillet, and place in oven until hot. Be sure to use a dry pot holder when removing the hot skillet from the oven; if it's even slightly damp, the steam will come through the cloth and burn you.

Bake at 400° until golden brown. The amount of time depends on what type pans you use. It takes about 15 to 20 minutes in muffin tins, and 35 to 40 minutes in larger pans. As in testing cakes, use a toothpick to test for doneness.

Yield: 12-15 servings

Low-Fat Buttermilk Cornbread

2 cups self-rising cornmeal
2 tablespoons vegetable oil
1 1/2 cups buttermilk
1 egg

Combine cornmeal, oil, buttermilk, and egg in bowl; mix well. Pour a small amount of additional oil into cast-iron skillet; preheat skillet in 450° oven. Sprinkle a small amount of cornmeal over bottom of skillet. Pour in cornmeal batter. Bake at 475° for 15 to 20 minutes or until golden brown.

Yield: 8 servings

Mexican Cornbread

1½ cups self-rising cornmeal
1¼ cups shredded cheddar cheese
2 eggs
1 cup grated onion
4 medium to large hot peppers, chopped
¼ cup vegetable oil, heated
1¼ cups milk

Combine cornmeal, cheese, eggs, onion, and hot peppers in bowl. Add oil and milk; mix well. Pour into hot greased cast-iron skillet. Bake at 375° for 45 minutes or until golden brown.

Yield: 8 servings

Buttermilk Mexican Cornbread

1½ cups self-rising cornmeal
1 large onion, chopped
1 (8-ounce) can cream-style corn
1½ cups shredded cheddar cheese
4 to 6 jalapeno peppers, chopped
2 eggs, beaten
¼ cup oil
1 to 1½ cups buttermilk

Combine cornmeal, onion, corn, cheese, and jalapeno peppers in bowl. Add eggs, oil, and enough buttermilk to make batter of desired consistency. Pour into hot greased 8 x 8-inch pan. Bake at 375° for 1 hour.

Yield: 8 servings

Sour Cream Cornbread

2 cups self-rising meal
½ cup vegetable oil
1 cup sour cream
1 (8-ounce) can cream-style corn
2 eggs, beaten

Combine all ingredients in bowl; mix well. Pour into hot greased 8-inch cast-iron skillet. Bake at 450° for 20 minutes or until brown.

Yield: 8 servings

A friend loveth at all times.

— PROVERBS 17:17 KJV —

Chapter 5

Irondale Cafe Specialties

Appetizers

Dips and Dressings

Sauces and Gravies

Condiments

Desserts

Appetizers

If you want to be respected by others the greatest thing you can do is respect yourself.

— ANONYMOUS —

Butterfly Wieners

1 or 2 pounds wieners, all beef
1 tablespoon oil
1½ cups barbecue sauce

Cut each wiener into four equal pieces; cut an X in both ends of each piece. Place wieners in a skillet with oil and cook over medium heat until ends flare; drain juices. Place wieners in a pan with the barbecue sauce and bake at 350° for 25 to 30 minutes.

Yield: 6-8 servings

Chicken Wings

2 pounds chicken wings
garlic salt or powder
½ cup cornstarch
1 egg, beaten
¾ cup sugar
1½ cups red wine vinegar
1 tablespoon soy sauce
¼ cup ketchup
1 teaspoon salt

Rinse chicken wings and pat dry. Separate at joint and reserve tips; place in a saucepan and cover with water. Boil until tender, discard tips and reserve ¼ cup broth. Add salt and roll in cornstarch. Dip wings in egg and place in a nonstick skillet; fry until wings are browned on both sides. Remove from skillet and place in baking pan.

Combine reserved broth, sugar, vinegar, soy sauce, ketchup, and salt in saucepan; mix well. Cook until sugar dissolves, stirring frequently. Pour mixture over chicken wings and bake at 350° for 30 minutes.

Yield: 24 servings

Cheese Balls

1 pound sharp cheddar cheese, grated
2 cups flour
½ cup margarine
½ teaspoon red pepper

Combine all ingredients and blend well. Form dough into ½-inch balls and bake at 400° until golden brown.

Yield: 25 servings

Refrigerated Cheese Wafers

½ cup butter, softened
1 cup self-rising flour, sifted
1 teaspoon salt
½ teaspoon red pepper
½ cup chopped pecans
2 cups shredded sharp cheddar cheese

Cream butter with a mixer until light and fluffy. Add flour, salt, red pepper, pecans, and cheese; mix well. Shape dough into a 1-inch roll and wrap in waxed paper; chill until firm. Slice dough and place on baking sheet. Bake at 325° for 10 minutes. Let cool on wire rack.

Yield: 40 servings

Easy Cheese Ball

8 ounces cream cheese, softened
8 ounces medium cheddar cheese, shredded, at room temperature
1 clove garlic, finely chopped
paprika
assorted crackers

Combine cream cheese, cheddar cheese, and garlic; shape into a ball. Garnish with paprika and serve with assorted crackers.

Yield: 16 servings

Nutty Cheese Ball

16 ounces cream cheese, softened
¼ cup finely chopped onion
½ cup chopped green pepper
2 cups chopped pecans
1 tablespoon seasoned salt
1 (8-ounce) can crushed pineapple, drained
assorted crackers

Combine all ingredients, reserving 1 cup pecans; shape into a ball. Chill until firm, and roll ball in reserved pecans. Serve with assorted crackers.

Yield: 16 servings

Party Cheese Ball

1 (8-ounce) package cream cheese, at room temperature
¾ cup crumbled blue cheese
1 cup shredded sharp cheddar cheese
¼ cup minced onion
1 tablespoon Worcestershire sauce
parsley, finely chopped
small crisp crackers

Combine cream cheese, blue cheese, cheddar cheese, onion, and Worcestershire sauce and beat with a mixer on low speed. When mixture is blended, increase to medium speed until mixture is fluffy. Shape mixture into 1 large or 36 small balls. Roll ball(s) in parsley and place on a serving plate. Chill covered, for 2 hours or until firm. Arrange crackers around cheese ball and serve.

Yield: 10-12 servings

Sausage Balls

1 pound pork sausage
⅓ cup breadcrumbs
½ teaspoon sage
1 egg, beaten
½ cup ketchup
2 tablespoons brown sugar
1 tablespoon soy sauce
1 tablespoon vinegar

Combine sausage, breadcrumbs, sage, and egg in bowl; mix well and shape into 1-inch balls. Place balls in skillet and cook over low heat until browned; drain. Combine ketchup, brown sugar, soy sauce, and vinegar; pour over sausage balls and mix well. Let simmer for 15 to 20 minutes.

Yield: 32 servings

Stuffed Jalapeno Peppers

16 jalapeno peppers, seeded
8 ounces cream cheese, cubed
2 eggs, beaten
1 cup flour

Stuff each pepper with cream cheese. Combine eggs and flour; roll each pepper in mixture. Place peppers in a deep-fryer and brown; drain peppers on a paper towel.

Yield: 16 servings

Wrapped Livers

12 chicken livers, halved
12 slices bacon, cut lengthwise
24 water chestnuts

Rinse livers and pat dry; wrap bacon around each liver and place 1 water chestnut in each; secure with wooden toothpick and place on baking sheet. Broil 5-8 minutes until bacon is crisp; drain livers. Turn livers and broil an additional 5-8 minutes.

Yield: 24 servings

Dips and Dressings

From acquaintances, we conceal our real selves.
To our friends, we reveal our weaknesses.

— BASIL HUME —

Fat-free Spinach Dip

- 1 (10-ounce) package frozen chopped spinach, thawed and drained
- 1 (8-ounce) can chopped water chestnuts, drained
- 1 (8-ounce) container fat-free sour cream
- 1 (8-ounce) container fat-free plain yogurt
- 1 envelope dry vegetable or onion soup mix
- 1 scallion, finely chopped

Combine all ingredients, place in a covered container and refrigerate.

Note: Spinach dip is better if made a couple of hours before serving.

Yield: about 12 servings

Fat-free White Bean Dip

- 1 (20-ounce) can white beans, drained
- 2 large cloves garlic, minced
- ½ teaspoon coarsely ground white pepper
- 1 tablespoon lemon juice
- fat-free crackers

Combine all ingredients in a blender and blend until smooth. Serve with fat-free crackers.

Yield: approximately 1 cup

Sweet Dip

- 1 (3-ounce) package cream cheese, softened
- 1 (7-ounce) jar marshmallow creme
- 1 tablespoon orange peel
- dash of ginger

Mix all ingredients and serve with fresh fruit.

Yield: 1¼ cups

Hacienda Dip

2 (8-ounce) packages cream cheese, softened
½ cup salsa
dash of onion salt
corn chips or vegetables

Mix cream cheese, salsa, and onion salt until well blended; place in a microwavable pie plate or bowl. Microwave on HIGH 3 to 4 minutes or until thoroughly heated, stirring every 2 minutes.

Serve with corn chips or vegetables.

Yield: 2 cups

Fish Dip

1 can light tuna, drained (tuna in spring water is best)
1 package onion soup mix
1 (16-ounce) container sour cream
chips or saltines

Combine first 3 ingredients; mix well and chill. Serve with chips or saltines.

Yield: 1½ pints

The Best Celery Stuffing

½ cup crumbled blue cheese
12 ounces cottage cheese (creamed small curd)
¼ cup mayonnaise
¼ teaspoon pepper
1 teaspoon seasoned salt
1 teaspoon garlic powder
½ cup grated cheddar cheese

Mix all ingredients until well blended using a fork (mixture is thick). Refrigerate in an airtight container.

Note: For a lighter version, I use low-fat cottage cheese and light mayonnaise. It's still good enough to eat!

Yield: 1½ pints

Blue Cheese Dressing

½ cup crumbled blue cheese
16 ounces sour cream
2 tablespoons mayonnaise
1 teaspoon seasoned salt
1 teaspoon garlic powder
½ teaspoon pepper

Combine blue cheese and sour cream, mashing blue cheese while mixing. Add mayonnaise and seasonings; mix well, whipping lightly with a fork. Refrigerate in an airtight container.

Note: This is wonderful on tossed salads, as a dip for raw vegetables, and instead of ketchup with French fries.

Note: For a lighter version, use light sour cream and light mayonnaise. I don't like "fat-free" mayonnaise, but the "light" has a good flavor.

Yield: 1¼ pints

1000 Island Salad Dressing

1 cup ketchup
¾ cup mayonnaise
⅓ cup sweet pickle relish

Combine all ingredients and mix with a large spoon until mixture is salmon colored. Cover and refrigerate.

Note: For a lighter version I use:

1 cup ketchup
¾ cup light mayonnaise
⅓ cup dill pickle relish
1 tablespoon pickle juice
Pretty good!

Yield: 2 cups

Tomato Dressing

½ cup tomato puree
1 cup low-fat cottage cheese
¼ cup skim milk
2 scallions, chopped
1 teaspoon fresh chives

Combine all ingredients and place in a blender; puree for 1 minute.

Yield: 2 cups

Green Goddess

10-12 fresh spinach leaves
5 sprigs fresh watercress
1-2 sprigs fresh parsley
1 teaspoon dried tarragon
1 small clove garlic (optional)
1 cup low-fat or fat-free plain yogurt
2 teaspoons fresh lemon juice
1/4 teaspoon coarsely ground white pepper

Combine all ingredients and place in a blender; puree for 1 minute.

Yield: 1 1/4 cups

Dill Dressing

1/2 cup nonfat yogurt
1/4 cup mock sour cream or commercial nonfat yogurt
2 teaspoons white wine vinegar
2 tablespoons fresh lemon juice
1/4 to 1/2 cup chopped fresh dill
1/4 to 1/2 teaspoon white pepper

Combine all ingredients and place in a blender; puree for 1 minute.

Yield: 1 1/4 cups

Apple Dressing

1/2 cup low or nonfat yogurt
1/4 cup sugar-free apple concentrate
1 tablespoon fresh lemon juice
1/2 teaspoon cinnamon
1/4 teaspoon nutmeg

Combine all ingredients and place in a blender; puree for 1 minute.

Yield: 3/4 cup

Herb Garden Dressing

1 medium clove garlic, mashed
¼ cup celery tops
½ cup fresh parsley
½ teaspoon white pepper
½ teaspoon chives
½ teaspoon dry mustard
½ teaspoon basil
½ teaspoon dill
½ cup fresh parsley
⅓ to ½ cup white wine or balsamic vinegar
¼ cup extra virgin olive oil
½ cup water
½ teaspoon tarragon
½ teaspoon paprika

Combine all ingredients in a shaker bottle and let stand at room temperature for several hours. Store in refrigerator.

Yield: approximately 1½ cups

Honey-Mustard Dressing

¼ cup extra virgin olive oil
¼ cup water
¼ cup white wine vinegar
3 tablespoons honey
1 tablespoon Dijon mustard

Combine all ingredients in a shaker bottle and refrigerate.

Yield: ¾ cup

Berry Dressing

¼ cup extra virgin olive oil
¼ cup water
¼ cup white wine vinegar
3-4 tablespoons seedless, sugarless raspberry, blueberry, or strawberry jam

Combine all ingredients and place in a blender; puree for 1 minute.

Yield: ¾ cup

Mock Sour Cream

1 can evaporated skim milk
2 teaspoons lemon juice
3 tablespoons fat-free plain yogurt

Refrigerate milk for several hours; place in a chilled bowl with lemon juice, and blend.

Fold in yogurt.

Yield: 2 cups

The best mirror is an old friend.

— GEORGE HERBERT —

Sauces and Gravies

My definition of a friend is one who knows all about you and won't go away.

— ANONYMOUS —

Barbecue Sauce

- 1 (3½-quart) bottle ketchup
- ½ gallon white vinegar
- 2 cups water
- ½ cup sugar
- 2 tablespoons salt
- 2 tablespoons black pepper
- ½ tablespoon cayenne pepper
- 2½ tablespoons barbecue spice
- juice of one lemon (drop rind into pot while cooking, and then remove it)

Mix all ingredients in a large stockpot and bring to a boil over high heat, stirring well. Reduce heat and simmer 1½ hours, stirring often. Pour into sterilized jars, and tighten lids (after cool). Store in refrigerator for several weeks.

Yield: 1½ gallons

Marinara Sauce

- ½ cup chopped onion
- 2 cloves garlic, minced
- 1 tablespoon olive oil
- 4 (14½-ounce) cans diced tomatoes (crushed tomatoes also work well)
- 2 tablespoons lemon juice
- 1 tablespoon dried Italian seasoning
- 2 bay leaves

Cook onion and garlic in olive oil in a Dutch oven over medium-high heat, stirring constantly, until tender. Add tomatoes and remaining ingredients. Bring to a boil; reduce heat to medium, (stirring occasionally) and cook 20 minutes or until most of the liquid evaporates. Remove from heat and discard bay leaves.

Yield: 5 cups

Spaghetti Sauce

- 2 pounds ground chuck
- 1 green bell pepper, chopped
- 1 onion, chopped
- 2 pieces celery from stalk, chopped
- 2 tablespoons oil
- 1 teaspoon salt
- ½ teaspoon pepper
- ½ teaspoon garlic powder
- 1 tablespoon oregano leaf
- 1 cup water
- 1 (29-ounce) can diced or crushed tomatoes with juice
- 1 (16-ounce) can tomato sauce
- 1 cup oats

Cook meat in a large skillet, stirring to crumble, until meat is almost done. Pour meat into a colander and let drain; rinse skillet with hot water to remove any fat. Return meat to skillet and add bell pepper, onion, celery, and spices. Stir well, adding 1 cup of water to mixture. Cover and let simmer 10 minutes; add tomatoes and tomato sauce, and stir well. Sprinkle oats over mixture, and stir well. Simmer over very low heat. (The oats will thicken the sauce).

Yield: 2¾ quarts

Note: If you have leftovers, mix the meat sauce with cooked spaghetti, stirring well. Place in a casserole dish, and refrigerate. Heat, covered, at 375° for about 30 minutes; uncover, sprinkle with shredded cheddar cheese and Parmesan cheese, and bake an additional 10 minutes.

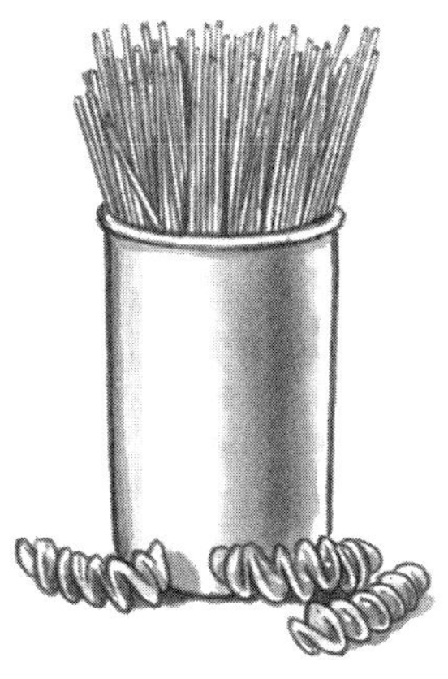

Creamy Parmesan Cheese Sauce

1 (8-ounce) package cream cheese, cubed
3/4 cup milk
1/2 cup (2 ounces) grated Parmesan cheese
dash of ground nutmeg and pepper
3 1/2 cups hot cooked pasta

Combine cream cheese, milk, and Parmesan cheese in a 1-quart casserole dish. Microwave on medium (50% power) 6 to 8 minutes or until sauce is smooth, stirring every 2 minutes. Stir in seasonings. Toss with hot cooked pasta.

Yield: 2 cups

Tomato Béarnaise Sauce

2 tablespoons white wine vinegar
2 tablespoons dry white wine
2 teaspoons chopped fresh tarragon or 1 teaspoon dried leaf tarragon
2 medium shallots, finely chopped
4 egg yolks
1/2 teaspoon salt
1/2 teaspoon coarsely cracked pepper
1 tablespoon tomato paste
1 cup unsalted butter

Pour boiling water into a 1-pint wide thermos jar to keep warm. Heat the first 4 ingredients in a small saucepan until almost all liquid is absorbed. Place shallot mixture in a blender or a food processor fitted with a steel blade. Add egg yolks, salt, pepper, and tomato paste; blend 20 seconds.

Heat butter in same pan until sizzling hot, but not browned. Slowly pour hot butter into blender or food processor in a thin stream while the motor is on. Taste for seasoning.

Drain and dry thermos jar, and immediately pour in hot sauce. This will keep the sauce hot for up to 30 minutes. Serve hot.

Yield: 1 1/2 cups

Blender Hollandaise Sauce

3 egg yolks
2 tablespoons lemon juice
dash of cayenne pepper
½ cup margarine or butter

Place egg yolks, lemon juice, and pepper in a blender and cover; quickly turn blender on and off. Heat margarine until melted and almost boiling. Turn blender on high speed; slowly pour in margarine, blending until thick and fluffy, about 30 seconds. Heat over warm (not hot) water until ready to serve.

Yield: 1 cup

White Sauce

2 tablespoons butter
2 tablespoons all-purpose flour
¼ teaspoon salt
¼ teaspoon white pepper
1 cup milk

Melt butter in saucepan over low heat. Blend in remaining ingredients, stirring constantly, until mixture bubbles. Remove from heat and serve immediately. To thicken sauce, increase butter and flour by one tablespoon.

Yield: 1½ cups

New Orleans Rémoulade Sauce

2 cups fresh mayonnaise
1 teaspoon grated onion
1 clove garlic, finely minced
½ cup Creole mustard
1 cup finely chopped parsley

Combine all ingredients, mix well. Use as a sauce for chilled, cooked shrimp.

Yield: enough sauce for 3 pounds of shrimp

Sweet and Sour Sauce

1 cup sugar
½ cup white vinegar
½ cup water
1 tablespoon chopped bell pepper
1 tablespoon chopped pimento
½ teaspoon salt
2 teaspoons cornstarch
1 tablespoon cold water
1 teaspoon paprika

Combine first 6 ingredients in saucepan and simmer over low heat for five minutes. Combine cornstarch and cold water and add to hot mixture. Cook until sauce thickens. Add paprika and serve with shrimp.

Yield: 1½ cups

Chicken Gravy

- 1/4 cup drippings from fried chicken
- 1/4 cup self-rising flour
- 2 cups milk
- salt and pepper
- biscuits, mashed potatoes, or cooked rice

Fry chicken in large skillet, reserving 1/4 cup drippings for gravy. Sprinkle 1/2 cup self-rising flour over drippings and stir well with fork. When flour begins to brown slightly, stir in 2 cups whole milk. Let gravy cook until thickened, sprinkle with salt and pepper. Pour over biscuits, mashed potatoes, or cooked rice.

Note: To make sawmill gravy, use bacon or sausage drippings, and add 1 cup milk and 1 cup water to 1/2 cup flour and stir with a whisk until flour is blended with the water.

Yield: 2 1/2 cups

Billy's Cocktail Sauce

- 2 cups ketchup
- juice of 1 lemon
- 1/2 cup freshly-ground horseradish
- 2 tablespoons Worcestershire sauce

Combine all ingredients and place in a fruit jar; refrigerate. Stir well before use.

Yield: 2 1/2 cups

Whenever we can we should always be kind to everyone.

— GALATIANS 6:10 TLB —

Condiments

Basil or Mint Jelly

2 cups water
1 cup vinegar
1 cup basil or mint leaves
green vegetable coloring (optional)
$6\frac{1}{2}$ cups sugar
1 bottle fruit pectin

Combine water, vinegar, basil or mint leaves, coloring, and sugar in a saucepan; heat to boiling. Add fruit pectin; heat to rolling boil, and cook 1 minute. Remove leaves. Seal jelly in hot sterilized jars.

Yield: 7 cups

Jalapeno Jelly

$\frac{3}{4}$ cup finely chopped, seeded jalapeno peppers
$\frac{3}{4}$ cup finely chopped green bell pepper
$1\frac{1}{2}$ cups vinegar
$6\frac{1}{2}$ cups sugar
2 (6-ounce) packages liquid fruit pectin

Combine peppers, vinegar, and sugar in a large boiler; bring to a boil. Reduce heat; simmer, uncovered, 5 minutes. Add fruit pectin; mix well, and bring to a boil. Reduce heat, and simmer 4 minutes.

Quickly pour jelly into sterilized jars, leaving $\frac{1}{4}$-inch headspace; cover at once with metal lids, and screw band tightly. Process in a boiling water bath for 5 minutes.

Yield: 6 cups

Old-fashioned Corn Relish

- 1/4 cup sugar
- 1/2 cup cider vinegar
- 1/2 teaspoon salt
- 1/4 teaspoon hot sauce
- 1/2 teaspoon celery seed
- 1/4 teaspoon mustard seed
- 1 (12-ounce) can whole-kernel corn, drained
- 2 tablespoons chopped green bell pepper
- 1 tablespoon chopped pimento
- 1 tablespoon minced onion

Combine sugar, vinegar, salt, hot sauce, celery seed, and mustard seed in saucepan; bring to a boil and cook for 2 minutes. Remove from heat, combine with remaining ingredients, and refrigerate.

Yield: 1 2/3 cups

Cranberry Orange Relish

- 5 cups fresh cranberries
- 2 cups sugar
- 1 cup orange juice
- 1/2 cup finely chopped orange rind
- 1/2 teaspoon ground nutmeg
- 1/2 teaspoon ground cardamom

Combine all ingredients in a heavy saucepan, and stir well. Bring to a boil; reduce heat and simmer (stirring occasionally) for 10 minutes or until cranberries pop. Remove from heat and let cool. Pour into a serving bowl and refrigerate.

Note: This relish is delicious with meats and dressing.

Yield: 4 cups

Pickled Peaches

1 cup sugar
1 cup cider vinegar
1 cup water
12 peaches, peeled
cloves (24 pieces)

Combine sugar, vinegar, and water in saucepan; bring to a boil and cook until sugar dissolves. Stick 2 cloves into each peach; add peaches to syrup mixture and cook until soft. Pack peaches in jars; cover with syrup, and seal. Store in refrigerator.

Yield: 3 quarts or 12 servings

Pickled Okra

2 pounds small okra
4 tablespoons dillweed
4 garlic cloves
3 cups vinegar
1½ cups water
½ cup salt

Trim tough stems from okra pods; do not cut into pods. Pack into sterilized pint jars, adding 1 table-spoon dillweed and 1 clove of garlic to each jar.

Mix vinegar, water, and salt in saucepan; bring to a boil. Pour over okra; seal jars. Let stand for 3 weeks to ripen; chill before serving.

Yield: 4 pints

Desserts

Banana Split Cake

- 3 sticks margarine, 1 melted and 2 softened
- 2 cups graham cracker crumbs
- 3 cups sifted confectioners' sugar
- 1/3 cup Half & Half
- 5 medium or 3 large bananas
- 1 (15-ounce) can pineapple tidbits in its own syrup
- 1 large container Cool Whip or Lite Cool Whip
- 1/2 cup chocolate syrup
- 1/2 cup chopped pecans
- 1/2 cup chopped maraschino cherries

Combine 1 stick melted margarine and graham cracker crumbs; mix well and pack into a 9 x 13-inch pan or Pyrex dish. Refrigerate crust.

Combine 2 sticks soft margarine, confectioners' sugar, and Half & Half in mixing bowl; beat at medium speed for 10 minutes. Spread filling over chilled crust. Cut bananas into 1/4-inch thick slices and place into filling, pressing slightly. Drain pineapple tidbits, and chop into smaller pieces; spread on top of bananas. Top with Cool Whip and freeze.

Remove from freezer 1 hour before serving and garnish with chocolate syrup, chopped pecans, and maraschino cherries.

Note: If all of the cake is not used, spread a coat of Cool Whip over exposed area covering bananas well; cover tightly and store in freezer for up to 3 weeks.

Note: This recipe was given to me by a friend 15 years ago. The original recipe called for 2 raw eggs and crushed pineapple, but since the scare of salmonella in raw eggs, we switched to Half & Half for the filling. Also, because crushed pineapple retains some of the juice even after draining, it tends to make the cake watery. We switched to tidbits because you can get more of the juice out of them. After draining, press with a spoon to squeeze out more juice; chop the tidbits and drain again. This may take a little more time, but it sure does make the dessert taste better and last longer.

Raw Apple Cake

½ cup shortening
2 cups sugar
2 eggs
2 cups flour
1 teaspoon ginger
2 teaspoons soda
½ teaspoon salt
2 teaspoons cinnamon
1 cup raisins (optional)
1 cup chopped black walnuts or a mixture of English walnuts and pecans
4 cups tart apples, thinly sliced

Cream together shortening, sugar, and eggs. Add flour, ginger, soda, salt, and cinnamon; mix well. Fold in raisins, nuts, and apples.

Bake in a 9 x 12-inch greased and floured pan at 350° for 50 minutes.

Applesauce Cake

1 cup butter or margarine
2 cups brown sugar
2 eggs
2 cups applesauce
1 cup raisins
1 cup chopped pecans
2 ½ cups all purpose flour
1 teaspoon baking powder
½ teaspoon baking soda
¼ teaspoon salt
1 teaspoon cinnamon
1 teaspoon allspice
1 teaspoon nutmeg

Cream together butter, sugar, and eggs. Add applesauce, raisins, and nuts.

Sift together all dry ingredients; add to other mixture 1 cup at a time, stirring well after each addition.

Bake in a 9 x 12-inch greased and floured pan at 375° for 30 minutes.

Red Velvet Cake

- ¼ pound butter or margarine, softened
- 1½ cups sugar
- 3 large eggs
- 1 teaspoon baking soda
- 1 cup buttermilk
- 2 tablespoons unsweetened cocoa
- 1 tablespoon red food coloring mixed with 1 teaspoon vanilla
- 2 cups all-purposc flour mixcd with ½ teaspoon salt and ¼ teaspoon baking powder
- 1 tablespoon cider vinegar

With electric mixer, cream together butter and sugar until light. Add eggs one at a time, and continue to beat. Add baking soda to buttermilk. Alternately add cocoa, food coloring mixture, flour mixture, and buttermilk mixture to batter. When batter is well mixed, add vinegar. With spatula, transfer to 2 lightly greased 9-inch cake pans and bake at 350° about 25 minutes. Remove from pans; cool on wire racks.

Cream Cheese Frosting

- ¼ pound softened butter
- 8 ounces softened cream cheese
- 1 teaspoon vanilla
- 1 (1-pound) box confectioners' sugar

Cream together butter and cream cheese; add vanilla and confectioners' sugar, mixing well. Frost cool cake layers.

Easy Red Velvet Cake

1 box Butter Recipe cake mix
1 teaspoon cocoa
1 teaspoon vanilla
1 cup buttermilk
1 ounce red food coloring
1 stick margarine, softened
3 eggs
1 teaspoon soda
1 teaspoon vinegar

Combine cake mix and cocoa; mix well. Add vanilla, buttermilk, food coloring, margarine, and eggs, beating until well moistened. Add soda and vinegar; beat at medium speed for 5 minutes.

Bake in 2 greased and floured 9-inch pans at 375° for 25 to 30 minutes or until done. When layers are cool, frost with cream cheese frosting.

Peanut Butter Apple Muffins

1 1/4 cup all-purpose flour, sifted
1/2 cup whole-wheat flour, sifted
4 teaspoons baking powder
3/4 teaspoon salt
1/2 teaspoon cinnamon
1/4 teaspoon nutmeg
2 tablespoons peanut oil
1/4 cup unsalted creamy peanut butter
1/4 cup sugar
1 egg
1 cup skim milk
3/4 cup apple, chopped
2 tablespoons sugar mixed with 1/4 teaspoon cinnamon

Sift together flours, baking powder, salt, cinnamon, and nutmeg; set aside. Cream oil and peanut butter with sugar, beating until light and fluffy. Add egg, and beat well. Stir in milk and chopped apple. Add flour mixture and stir until dry ingredients are moistened. Fill greased or paper-lined muffin tins two-thirds full, and sprinkle top of batter with sugar-cinnamon mixture. Bake at 400° for 20 to 25 minutes.

Yield: 10-12 servings

Special Angel Food Cake

- Angel Food cake mix
- 1 can crushed pineapple in its own juice
- 1 (3-ounce) box instant sugar-free vanilla pudding mix
- 1 (16-ounce) container Lite Cool Whip

Bake cake mix according to package directions; let cool, and cut into 3 layers. Empty can of pineapple into a large mixing bowl. Sprinkle pudding mix over pineapple and mix well. Refrigerate for 40 minutes to 1 hour. Fold in Cool Whip; stir well. Spread between layers and on top of cake.

Note: Absolutely delicious and reduced in calories, too!

Delicious White Cake

- 2/3 cup shortening
- 2 cups sugar
- 1 teaspoon vanilla extract
- 2 3/4 cups high-quality all-purpose flour
- 1/2 teaspoon salt
- 1 tablespoon baking powder
- 1 cup water
- 4 egg whites
- 1/4 teaspoon cream of tartar

Thoroughly cream together shortening and sugar; add vanilla. Sift flour with salt and baking powder; add to creamed mixture alternating with water, beating well after each addition. Combine egg whites and cream of tartar; beat until stiff peaks form. Fold into mixture. Pour batter into 2 greased and floured 9-inch cake pans. Bake at 350° for 18 to 20 minutes.

Mississippi Mud Cake

1 1/4 cups sifted cake flour
2 teaspoons baking powder
1/8 teaspoon salt
2 cups sugar
3/4 cup cocoa
5 eggs, separated
1 cup cold water
1 teaspoon vanilla
3 cups miniature marshmallows

Sift together flour, baking powder, and salt; sift a second time. Combine sugar and cocoa in a large bowl. Beat egg yolks until thick; add to sugar mixture. Add water and vanilla; stir well. Add half the flour mixture; stir 50 strokes. Add remaining flour mixture; stir 50 strokes.

Beat egg whites until stiff peaks form; gently fold into batter with 20 to 25 strokes.

Pour into a greased and floured 9 x 12-inch baking dish or pan. Bake at 350(for 25 to 30 minutes.

Just as cake is done, remove from oven and spread miniature marshmallows all over top. Put back in oven just long enough for marshmallows to start melting and puffing up.

Remove from oven and cool. Ice with Dark Chocolate Icing below.

Note: You may substitute a Devil's Food cake mix for the above cake recipe.

Dark Chocolate Icing

1 (8-ounce) box unsweetened baking chocolate
1/3 pound margarine
2 tablespoons cornstarch
2 cups water
4 cups confectioners' sugar
chopped pecans (optional)

Combine chocolate and margarine in saucepan; heat over low heat to melt. Place cornstarch in another saucepan and add water, a little at a time, until cornstarch is dissolved. Heat over low heat until mixture starts to thicken; remove from heat and add to melted chocolate and margarine, blending well. Add confectioners' sugar and stir until sugar is dissolved and mixture is smooth. Sprinkle chopped pecans over cake, if desired.

Note: This makes more than enough icing to cover cake; store leftover icing in the refrigerator.

Best-Ever Coconut Cake

Delicious White Cake (page 142)
evaporated milk
1 pint whipping cream
½ cup confectioners' sugar
1¾ cup finely shredded coconut

Mix Delicious White Cake and bake in a 9 x 13-inch pan at 350° for 25 to 30 minutes. Let cool; punch holes about 3 inches apart with end of beaters, and pour evaporated milk over top. Do not soak! A little evaporated milk goes a long way.

Combine whipping cream, and confectioners' sugar; whip until stiff peaks form. Fold in 1 cup coconut and spread mixture over cake. Sprinkle ¾ cup finely shredded coconut on top.

Note: If you prefer a layer cake, bake cake in 2 greased and floured 9-inch cake pans. Follow same process, being careful not to saturate layers.

Note: This cake can be frozen for later use. Be sure to take out of freezer an hour or so before slicing.

Variations

Using the above recipe, bake layers, using Lemon or Pineapple Surprise Filling on the following page, between layers. Yummy!

Don't let the sun go down on your anger.

— EPHESIANS 4:26 RSV —

Lemon Filling

- $1\frac{1}{4}$ cup sugar
- $\frac{1}{4}$ cup cornstarch
- 1 cup plus 2 tablespoons hot water
- 2 egg yolks, beaten
- 2 tablespoons margarine
- 1 tablespoon grated lemon peel
- 3 tablespoons lemon juice

Combine sugar and cornstarch in saucepan; add hot water, stirring to dissolve sugar and cornstarch. Stir in egg yolks; cook over medium heat until mixture thickens, stirring constantly.

Remove from heat; add margarine, lemon peel, and lemon juice, and continue to stir until margarine is melted and mixture is smooth. Spread filling between cake layers.

Pineapple Surprise Filling

- 1 small package instant vanilla pudding mix
- 1 can crushed pineapple, undrained
- 1 pint whipping cream, whipped stiff

Combine dry pudding mix with pineapple. Refrigerate for about 1 hour; fold in whipped cream.

Spread filling between layers and on top of cake.

Note: Especially good!

Green Tomato Pie

6 cups (1/8-inch thick) slices unpeeled green tomatoes
boiling water
1 cup sugar
1/4 teaspoon salt
3 tablespoons flour
1/4 teaspoon ground nutmeg
1/4 teaspoon cinnamon
2 tablespoons butter
juice and grated rind of 1 lemon
pastry for 2-crust 9-inch pie

Place tomato slices in a bowl and cover with boiling water. Let stand 3 minutes; drain. Combine sugar, salt, flour, and spices in a small bowl. Combine lemon juice and rind in another bowl. Fill pastry-lined pie plate with layers of green tomato slices, sprinkling each layer with sugar mixture, pats of butter, and small amount of lemon mix. Cover filling with pastry in a lattice pattern. Bake at 450° for 8 to 10 minutes; reduce heat to 375° and bake an additional 40 minutes or until tomatoes are tender.

Happiness is a perfume you cannot pour on others without getting a few drops on yourself.

— GEORGE BERNARD SHAW —

Chewy Tomato Bars

2 cups ground green tomatoes
juice and grated peel of 1 orange
1 teaspoon cinnamon
½ teaspoon salt
½ cup plus 2 tablespoons sugar
1 tablespoon lemon juice
¼ teaspoon cloves
½ cup chopped walnuts

Combine all ingredients except walnuts in a saucepan, and cook until most of liquid has evaporated and mixture is thick, stirring occasionally. Stir in walnuts. Pour into prepared crust and bake at 350° for 30 minutes; let cool.

Crust

½ cup butter
1 cup firmly packed brown sugar
2 teaspoons vanilla
1½ cups sifted whole-wheat flour
1 teaspoon baking powder
½ teaspoon baking soda
1 teaspoon salt
1 cup quick-cooking oats

Cream together butter, sugar, and vanilla. Sift together flour, baking powder, baking soda, and salt; stir into butter mixture until smooth. Add oats; blend thoroughly.

Grease and flour an 8 x 12-inch pan; press half of oat mixture firmly into pan and cover with filling.

Sprinkle remaining oat mixture over filling and press down.

Yield: 24 squares

Rice Pudding

- 1 cup sugar
- 3 eggs, beaten
- 1 ½ cups milk
- ½ cup margarine or butter, softened
- 1 teaspoon ground cinnamon
- 1 teaspoon vanilla
- 3 cups cooked rice
- 1 cup raisins
- 1 tablespoon margarine, melted

Combine sugar, eggs, milk, and margarine in mixing bowl; add cinnamon and vanilla and mix well. Add rice and raisins; mix well. Pour into lightly greased 9 x 9-inch baking dish, bake at 350° for 35 to 40 minutes. Drizzle 1 tablespoon melted margarine over top the last few minutes of baking time to make the top brown.

Yield: 8-10 servings

Black-Bottom Pie

- ½ cup sugar
- 1 tablespoon cornstarch
- 2 cups milk, scalded
- 4 beaten egg yolks
- 1 teaspoon vanilla
- 1 (6-ounce) bag semisweet chocolate pieces
- 1 baked (9-inch) pie shell
- 1 tablespoon (1 envelope) unflavored gelatin
- ¼ cup cold water
- 4 egg whites
- ½ cup sugar
- 1 cup heavy cream, whipped
- chocolate decorettes

Combine sugar and cornstarch. Slowly add scalded milk to beaten egg yolks; stir in sugar mixture. Cook and stir in top of double boiler until the custard coats a spoon; add vanilla. Remove 1 cup of the custard, add the chocolate pieces, and stir until melted. Pour in bottom of baked, cooled pie shell; chill. Soften gelatin in cold water; add to remaining hot custard and stir until dissolved. Chill until thickened.

Beat egg whites, adding ½ cup sugar gradually, until stiff peaks form; fold in custard-gelatin mixture. Pour over chocolate layer and chill until set. Garnish with whipped cream and chocolate decorettes.

Chocolate Fudge Pie

1½ cups sugar
3 tablespoons cocoa
1 stick butter, melted
3 eggs
1 teaspoon vanilla
1 (8-inch) unbaked pie shell

Combine sugar and cocoa, add butter, eggs, and vanilla. Mix well and pour into pie shell. Bake at 350° for 35 minutes. Let cool for 10 minutes. Serve warm with ice cream or whipped cream.

Light Banana Pie

10 graham crackers
1 large banana
1 small box instant vanilla or banana sugar-free pudding mix
skim milk
Lite Cool Whip

Line 10-inch pie plate with graham crackers. Slice one large banana and place on top of graham crackers. Prepare instant sugar-free pudding according to directions, using skim milk, and pour over bananas. Top with Lite Cool Whip. Refrigerate until firm.

Light Side Banana Cream Pie

1 small box instant vanilla or banana sugar-free pudding mix
1 cup plain yogurt
2 cups Lite Cool Whip
¼ cup skim milk
sliced bananas

Combine pudding mix, yogurt, and milk; fold in Cool Whip. Beat with a wire whisk until well blended. Place half of mixture into pie plate; top with sliced bananas and remaining mixture. Refrigerate until firm.

Note: You can use a graham cracker crust for this recipe. Combine 1½ cups crushed graham crackers with ⅓ cup melted light margarine and press into pie plate. Crust will be thin.

Light Chocolate Pie

10 graham crackers
1 small box instant chocolate sugar-free pudding mix
Lite Cool Whip

Line 9-inch pie plate with graham crackers. Mix pudding and gently pour over crackers, being careful not to move crackers. (You can use a large spoon to cover the crackers while you pour the pudding.) Refrigerate until firm; spread Lite Cool Whip over pudding. Great!

Note: Graham crackers have a few less calories and a bit less fat than vanilla wafers.

Lemon Icebox Meringue Pie

1 can sweetened condensed milk
½ cup fresh lemon juice
2 large eggs, separated
grated rind of 1 lemon
½ teaspoon lemon extract
¼ teaspoon cream of tartar
2 tablespoons sugar
1 (8-inch) graham cracker pie shell

Blend milk, juice, egg yolks, grated rind, and lemon extract until mixture thickens. Beat egg whites and cream of tartar until stiff. Gradually add sugar, folding into egg whites. Spread over pie shell and bake at 350° about 10 minutes until golden brown. Chill before serving.

Note: Use Key lime juice instead of lemon juice to make Key Lime Icebox Pie.

Lemon Meringue Pie

- 1½ cups sugar
- ⅓ cup cornstarch
- ¼ teaspoon salt
- 2 cups cold water
- ½ cup lemon juice
- 3 eggs, separated
- 2 tablespoons butter or margarine
- ½ tablespoon lemon rind, grated
- 1 (8-inch) baked pie shell
- ¼ teaspoon cream of tartar
- ⅓ cup sugar

Combine sugar, cornstarch, and salt in large saucepan; mix well. Gradually add water and lemon juice, stirring until mixture is smooth. Beat egg yolks until thick and lemon colored; gradually stir into lemon mixture. Add butter and cook over medium heat, stirring constantly. Remove from heat and stir in lemon rind; pour into pie shell.

Combine room temperature egg whites and cream of tartar; beat until foamy. Gradually add sugar, 1 tablespoon at a time, beating until stiff peaks form. Spread meringue over pie filling, sealing edges to pastry. Bake at 350° for 12 to 15 minutes or until golden brown. Let cool before cutting.

Sweet Potato Pie

- 4 eggs, separated
- 1½ cups sugar
- 3 cups cooked, mashed sweet potatoes
- ½ cup softened margarine or butter
- 2 cups milk
- 2 teaspoons vanilla extract
- 1 teaspoon ground nutmeg
- 1½ teaspoons ground cinnamon
- 2 (9-inch) unbaked pie shells

Beat egg yolks until thick. Gradually add sugar; mix well. Add next 6 ingredients and mix well.

Beat room temperature egg whites until stiff peaks form; fold into sweet potato mixture. Pour into pie shells and bake at 350° for 45 minutes or until set.

Rhubarb Pie

3 cups cut rhubarb
1 cup sugar
½ teaspoon grated orange peel
3 tablespoons flour
⅛ teaspoon salt
pastry for 2 crust (9-inch) pie
2 tablespoons butter or margarine

Combine rhubarb, sugar, orange peel, flour, and salt. Pour filling into pastry-lined pie plate; dot filling with butter and add top crust. Bake at 450° for 10 minutes; reduce heat to 350°, and bake an additional 30 minutes.

Pumpkin Pie

1½ cups cooked or canned pumpkin
¾ cup sugar
½ teaspoon salt
½ teaspoon ginger
1 teaspoon cinnamon
¼ teaspoon nutmeg
3 lightly beaten eggs
1¼ cups milk
1 (6-ounce) can evaporated milk or ¾ cup cream
pastry for 1 (9-inch) crust

Combine pumpkin, sugar, salt, and spices; mix well. Add eggs, milk, and evaporated milk or cream and blend well. Pour into pastry-lined pie plate. Bake at 450° for 10 minutes; reduce heat to 325° and bake an additional 45 minutes. Serve warm or cold, plain or topped with whipped cream.

Note: For an added attraction, combine ½ cup chopped pecans with 2 tablespoons brown sugar and sprinkle over top of pie during the last 15 minutes of baking.

Beth's Tart Lemon Pie

- 1 package sugar-free lemonade mix
- 1 package instant vanilla sugar-free pudding mix
- 2 cups skim milk
- 1 (12-ounce) container Light Cool Whip

Combine lemonade, pudding, and milk; fold in half of Cool Whip. Pour mixture into a ready-made 9-inch graham cracker crust. Top with remaining Cool Whip and chill 2 hours.

Yield: 6-8 servings

Pecan Pie

- 3 eggs
- 1 cup granulated or brown sugar
- 1 cup light corn syrup
- 1 cup pecan halves
- 1 teaspoon vanilla extract
- pastry for 1 (9-inch) crust

Beat eggs and sugar until thick; add corn syrup, pecans, and vanilla. Pour into pastry-lined pie plate; bake at 300° for 1 hour.

Note: You can sprinkle the pecans over the filling after pouring it into crust.

Old-fashioned Bread Pudding

- 4 cups breadcrumbs (leftover biscuits are wonderful to use)
- 4 eggs or 6 egg whites plus 2 yolks (save remaining yolks for Lemon Sauce), beaten
- 3 tablespoons margarine or butter, melted
- 3/4 cup sugar
- 3/4 cup raisins
- 1 teaspoon vanilla extract
- 2 cups milk

Place breadcrumbs in a large mixing bowl; pour milk over crumbs. Let stand a few minutes for bread to absorb milk. Add remaining ingredients, mixing well. Pour into a 13 x 9 x 2-inch lightly greased baking dish and bake at 325° for 45 to 50 minutes or until firm. Serve with hot Lemon Sauce or Magic Lemon Sauce (page 157) if desired.

Yield: 6 to 8 servings

Lemon Sauce

4 egg yolks, beaten
1/2 cup sugar
1/4 cup flour
1 1/2 cups milk
1/4 cup lemon juice

Combine yolks, sugar, flour, and milk in a saucepan; mix well. Cook over medium heat, stirring constantly, until thickened. Remove from heat, and stir in lemon juice. Serve hot.

Yield: 2 cups

Gingerbread

1/3 cup shortening, melted
2/3 cup boiling water
1 cup molasses
1 egg, beaten
2 2/4 cups all-purpose flour
1 1/2 teaspoons baking soda
1/2 teaspoon salt
1 teaspoon ground cinnamon
1 1/2 teaspoons ground ginger
1/4 teaspoon ground cloves

Combine shortening, water, molasses, and egg. Combine the dry ingredients; add to molasses mixture. Pour batter into a greased 9-inch square pan. Bake at 350° for 30 to 40 minutes or until a toothpick inserted in center comes out clean. Serve warm or room temperature with hot Lemon Sauce or *Magic Lemon Sauce* (page 157).

Glaze

1 cup confectioners' sugar
2 tablespoons boiling water
1/4 teaspoon vanilla

Place sugar in a bowl; add water and vanilla and stir rapidly until sugar melts. Whip until smooth. Spread on gingerbread while warm.

Note: You may need to add a little more water to spread the glaze thin.

RECIPES USING SWEETENED CONDENSED MILK

A friend gave me a booklet containing easy recipes made with sweetened condensed milk. From the looks of the booklet, it must be from the late twenties or early thirties. There may be updated versions of these recipes, but I have not seen them.

Caramelized Condensed Milk

A wonderful caramel pudding. It makes itself!

Place 1 can of sweetened condensed milk in kettle or large pot of boiling water and keep at boiling point for 3 hours. Caution: Be sure to keep the can covered with water.

Remove can from water and chill thoroughly.

Open can and serve as a wonderful pudding that has made itself, or use in the following recipes.

Note: You can boil several cans at the same time; when cool, store the cans in the refrigerator until you're ready to serve as pudding or use in a recipe. Remove the caramelized milk from can by immersing the can in hot water about 1 minute. Punch a hole in the bottom of can, remove the top of the can with a can opener and loosen the caramelized milk from the sides of the can with a knife dipped in hot water.

The most completely lost of all days is the one in which I have not laughed.

— ANONYMOUS —

Peanut Brittle Sauce

- 2/3 cup Caramelized Condensed Milk
- 1/2 cup hot water
- 1/2 pound crushed peanut brittle

Combine Caramelized Condensed Milk with hot water; beat until smooth. Add crushed peanut brittle. Serve over ice cream or cake.

Yield: 2 cups

Butterscotch Sauce

- 1 (14-ounce) can Caramelized Condensed Milk
- 1/2 cup dark corn syrup
- 1/2 cup butter or margarine

Combine corn syrup and butter in a saucepan, and bring to a boil. Remove from heat, and add caramelized condensed milk; beat until thoroughly blended. Mixture will thicken upon standing; blend it with water to desired consistency.

Yield: 2 cups

Caramel Bonbons

- 1 (14-ounce) can Caramelized Condensed Milk
- 3 cups confectioners' sugar, sifted
- 1 teaspoon vanilla
- 1 cup toasted coconut or chopped nuts

Combine caramelized milk and confectioners' sugar; add vanilla. Drop by teaspoonful onto toasted coconut or chopped nuts; form into patties or balls. Refrigerate.

Yield: 1 dozen

Magic Lemon Sauce

- 2/3 cup sweetened condensed milk
- 1/4 cup lemon juice
- 1 teaspoon grated lemon rind

Combine all ingredients, stirring well until mixture thickens. You can thin this sauce with water to desired consistency. It is great over warm Gingerbread or Old-fashioned Bread Pudding.

Yield: 1 cup

Chocolate Sauce

- 2 squares unsweetened chocolate
- 1 can sweetened condensed milk
- 1/8 teaspoon salt
- 1/2 to 1 cup hot water

Melt chocolate in a double boiler; add sweetened condensed milk, and stir over boiling water for 5 minutes or until mixture thickens. Add salt and hot water (amount depending on the consistency desired).

Note: To make Chocolate Peppermint Sauce, add 2 to 3 drops of peppermint oil.

Yield: 2 to 2½ cups

Don't walk in front of me, I may not follow.
Don't walk behind me, I may not lead.
Walk beside me and be my friend.

-ALBERT CAMUS-

Baked Custard

- 3/4 cup sweetened condensed milk
- 2 1/4 cups hot water
- 3 eggs, lightly beaten
- 1/4 teaspoon salt
- 1/4 teaspoon nutmeg

Combine sweetened condensed milk and hot water; slowly pour over eggs; add salt. Pour into a 9-inch round baking pan or custard cups; sprinkle with nutmeg. Place in a pan filled with hot water to depth of custard, and bake at 300° for 40 minutes or until custard is set. A knife blade inserted will come out clean when custard is done.

Note: You can use this recipe and make the following variations.

Yield: 6 servings

VARIATIONS

BAKED COCONUT CUSTARD: Add 3/4 to 1 cup shredded coconut.

COFFEE CUSTARD: Substitute 1 cup hot black coffee for 1 cup hot water.

NUT CUSTARD: Add 1/2 cup chopped nuts.

CHOCOLATE CUSTARD: Add 1 1/2 squares unsweetened chocolate, melted.

Fluff

Any flavor sugar-free Jell-O
1 (12-ounce) carton light cottage cheese
1 (15¾-ounce) can crushed pineapple in its own juice, well drained
1 (8-ounce) carton Lite Cool Whip

Combine Jell-O with cottage cheese: stir in pineapple. Add Lite Cool Whip, and stir well. Chill 2 hours.

Yield: 8-10 servings

Peach Fizz

3 medium unpeeled peaches, washed, pitted, and cut into pieces
2 teaspoons Crystal Light Lemonade mix dissolved in 1 cup cool water

Combine all ingredients in a blender; fill to top with crushed ice. Blend well. Serve immediately.

Yield: 2-3 servings

If someone is too tired to give you a smile, give him one of yours.

— ANONYMOUS —

Low-Fat Fruit Smoothies

Banana-Rama

1 ripe banana, peeled
1 cup skim milk
½ cup orange juice
½ cup pineapple chunks
1 teaspoon vanilla
1-2 tablespoons sugar
1-2 cups crushed ice

Combine all ingredients in a blender; blend at low speed for 1 minute.

Note: ½ cup plain yogurt can be added for a richer smoothie.

Yield: 2-3 servings

Just Berries

1 cup strawberries, blueberries, or blackberries
½ cup skim milk
1 cup sugar-free strawberry yogurt
1-2 cups crushed ice
1 pack sweetener

Combine all ingredients in a blender; blend at low speed for 1 minute.

Yield: 3-4 servings

Peach Tango

1 cup fresh or frozen peaches, sliced
1 cup sugar-free peach yogurt
1 kiwi, peeled and sliced
½ cup skim milk
1-2 cups crushed ice
1 tablespoon lemon juice
1 tablespoon sugar or sweetener

Combine all ingredients in a blender; blend at low speed for 1 minute.

Yield: 3 - 4 servings

Chapter 6

Tips for Healthier Eating

---

by

Connie F. McMichael, MS, RD

Tips for Healthier Eating

Connie F. McMichael, MS, RD

Why have a chapter on nutrition in a Southern cookbook? Although Southern food has traditionally been laden with fat and salt, a few recipes in this cookbook do not use lard or fatback like your grandmother may have used. Most of us do not eat home-cooked Southern foods every day, but traditional Southern cooking can fit into a diet by eating in moderation and making substitutions.

Healthy substitutions can be made in all your favorite recipes. It may surprise you that small changes can be just as tempting to the taste buds. You can make sensible changes without making tremendous sacrifices, especially today with all the reduced calorie, fat-free, and low sodium products.

Eating nutritiously can really make a difference in how you feel physically as well as mentally. Slowly making dietary changes is the key to successful long-term change in healthy living.

Shopping and Selecting Foods

When grocery shopping, first buy low-fat dairy products such as cheese, sour cream, milk, and margarine. After your taste buds have adjusted, change to fat-free versions of these products. Some fat-free products may not suit your taste buds at first; just continue to try different brands. Be careful of low-fat and fat-free dessert foods; they may be low in fat, but they are loaded with sugar. If these calories are not used, they are stored as body fat.

Choose lean meats that have less visible fat. Limit beef servings to three times a week. Buy fresh fish, chicken, and turkey because they are lower in fat than red meat.

Buy fresh vegetables when possible. The less fruits and vegetables have been processed, the more vitamins and minerals they retain. Always rinse fruits and vegetables before and after peeling to rid the food of pesticides and bacteria.

Never go to the grocery store hungry! Always take a grocery list with you to help reduce unnecessary spending.

Preparing and Cooking Foods

Before cooking meats, trim all visible fats. Bake, broil, boil, roast, or grill meats using the herbs and spices suggested in Chapter 2.

When preparing vegetables, do not use bacon grease or shortening. These are saturated fats that can lead to obesity and heart disease. Use herbs and spices, bouillon cubes, onions, peppers, and red potatoes while cooking to season the vegetables without adding fat. You can also use one teaspoon of vegetable oil or low-fat margarine. When cooking vegetables, use only small amounts of water so the vegetables will retain their natural vitamins and minerals. Steaming is also a great way to cook vegetables without the fat.

Buy fresh fruits when possible. If you buy fruit in the can, make sure the fruit is in its own juice with no added sugar. Fruits are naturally sweet; there is no need to add extra calories from sugar. Fruit drinks have added sugars and are not a healthy alternative to fruit juice.

Choosing a Diet Low in Fat and Cholesterol

There has been a lot of discussion on reducing the amount of fat in your diet. There are hundreds of different low-fat and low cholesterol products on the market. So why all the discussion on fat? Too much fat in the diet is related to obesity, heart disease, and cancer. Fat has more than twice the calories than carbohydrates and proteins. Our bodies are efficient and store extra calories in the form of fat. Although you need some fat in your diet, excess fat can be unhealthy and dangerous. There are three different types of fat.

Saturated Fat - Saturated fats are oils from animal products and some plants (coconut and palm) that are solid at room temperature. Examples are meat fat, butter, and shortening. These fats raise blood cholesterol which can increase your risk of heart disease. When reading a food label, the word hydrogenated should alert you that the fat may be saturated.

Polyunsaturated Fat - Polyunsaturated fats are vegetable oils and are liquid at room temperature. Examples are safflower oil and corn oil.

Monounsaturated Fat - Monounsaturated fats are oils from other vegetable products that are liquid at room temperature. Examples are olive oil and peanut oil.

Substituting polyunsaturated and monounsaturated fats in place of saturated fats can lower blood cholesterol and reduce your risk of heart disease. All fats should be used in moderation.

For more information, call the American Dietetic Association hot-line for consumers at **1-800-366-1655,** or contact a registered dietitian in your community.

HEALTHY ALTERNATIVES

COMMON CHOICES	HEALTHY ALTERNATIVES
Butter	Reduced calorie or nonfat margarine
Sour cream	Reduced calorie or nonfat sour cream, low-fat yogurt or cottage cheese
Bacon	Canadian bacon
Nondairy creamer	Skim milk or nonfat dry milk
Whole milk	Low-fat milk (1%) or skim milk
Salad dressing	Low or nonfat dressing, lemon juice, or herbs
Butter on vegetables	Cook with herbs, onion, half a potato, or bouillon cube
Cream or butter sauces	Sauces using wine or low-fat broth
Chocolate	Cocoa
Cooking with animal fats, bacon, lard, fatback	Cooking vegetables with a teaspoon of vegetable oil (safflower, canola, olive, or peanut)
Red meat every day	Lean red meat 3 times a week

HEALTHY ALTERNATIVES (continued)

COMMON CHOICES	HEALTHY ALTERNATIVES
One egg	Three egg whites or egg substitute
Oil in cake mix	Applesauce

Below is an example of how to make substitutions in your favorite recipes.

Zucchini Bread

3 eggs
2 cups sugar
1 cup oil
2 cups grated zucchini
1 tablespoon vanilla
3 cups flour
1 teaspoon baking soda
1/4 teaspoon baking powder
1 tablespoon cinnamon
1 cup chopped pecans

Pour into baking pan and bake 30 to 40 minutes (or until toothpick comes out clean) in a 375° oven.

- To reduce cholesterol, substitute 3 egg whites or 1/4 cup liquid egg substitute for every egg.
- Decrease sugar to 1 1/2 cups. The next time you use the recipe, cut the sugar to 1 cup.
- To reduce fat, try using 1/2 cup oil and 1/2 cup applesauce. Always use canola oil because it's lower in saturated fat than other oils.
- For extra fiber, do not peel zucchini. Use whole wheat flour instead of bleached flour.
- To reduce fat, use 1/2 cup chopped pecans instead of the whole cup.

A Special Thanks

We have had many employees during the last twenty-three years. Below are some of the names as well as a few friends who were good enough to help me when I was in a bind.

Babe
Barbara
Beth
Beth D.
Betty
Bill
Billie
Bobby
Brenda P.
Cindy
Connie
Darryl N.
Dwayne
Donnell
Doris M.
Doris V.
Frances
Genia
Ginny
Harry
James
James H.
James J.
Jane
Janette
Janiece
John
Josephine
Joyce
Judy
LaVoy
Lillie
Lillie J.
Linda
Lucy
Maisa
Margaret
Marie
Marilyn
Marjorie
Martha
Mary B.
Mary PLM
Ocie
Peanut
Raphael
Ray
Reda
Ruby
Sherry
Sue
Vanessa
Vickie
Zane

And in loving memory of

Miss Bess, Miss Sue, Lizzie, Carol, Rose M., Mildred C., Miss Bee, Henry, Gene, Helen, and our sweet Eva.

About the Author

Mary Jo Smith McMichael was born in Atlanta, Georgia, on May 24, 1932. The youngest of nine children, she graduated from high school in May 1949 and married Billy H. McMichael the following September. Mary Jo has three children: Billy, Jr., Mary Elizabeth (Beth), and Connie Frances. She and her husband reside in a suburb of Birmingham and continue to run the Irondale Cafe. She still finds time to be active in various civic groups and the Eastern Star. She is a member of the Methodist Church.

Mary Jo's Personal Philosophy

To awaken each morning with a smile brightening my face; to greet the day with reverence for the opportunities it contains; to approach my work with a clean mind; to hold ever before me, even in the doing of little things, the ultimate purpose toward which I am working; to meet men and women with laughter on my lips and love in my heart; to be gentle, kind, and courteous through all the hours; to approach the night with weariness that ever woos sleep and the joy that comes from work well done—this is how I desire to waste wisely my day.

-Thomas Dekker

Thank God every morning when you get up that you have something to do which must be done, whether you like it or not. Being forced to work, and forced to do your best, will breed in you temperance, self-control, diligence, strength of will, content, and a hundred other virtues which the idle never know.

-Charles Kingsley

We remember when Mom and Dad bought the Irondale Cafe. We remember how hard it was for her in the beginning because she knew nothing about the restaurant business, but she was an outstanding cook. We don't know of anyone who has worked harder than our mom; we often wondered where her strength came from. This cookbook is written by someone who is more than just a good cook; she is a wonderful person who has turned lemons into lemonade and has done so with dignity, love, and quiet pride. We hope you find the pleasure and love in this cookbook that we have had with Mary Jo McMichael as our mother.

Bill, Beth, and Connie

Now faith is the substance of things hoped for, the evidence of things not seen.

— HEBREWS 11:1 —